Truth, Knowledge, and Modality

Philosophical Papers of Georg Henrik von Wright
I   Practical Reason
II   Philosophical Logic
III   Truth, Knowledge, and Modality

Truth, Knowledge, and Modality

GEORG HENRIK VON WRIGHT

Philosophical Papers

Volume III

BASIL BLACKWELL

© G.H. von Wright 1984

First published 1984
Basil Blackwell Publisher Limited
108 Cowley Road, Oxford OX4 1JF, England

Basil Blackwell Inc.
432 Park Avenue South, Suite 1505,
New York, NY 10016, USA

British Library Cataloguing in Publication Data
Wright, G.H. von
Philosophical papers.
Vol.3: Truth, knowledge and modality
1. Philosophy
I. Title
192   B21

ISBN 0-631-13367-4

Typeset by MHL Typesetting Limited, Coventry
Printed in Great Britain by The Pitman Press Ltd., Bath

Contents

Introduction and Acknowledgements   vii

Determinism and Future Truth   1

Demystifying Propositions   14

Truth and Logic   26

    Truth-Logic and ''Dialectical Synthesis''   36

    Truth-Logic and Antinomies   39

The Logic of Predication   42

Determinism and Knowledge of the Future   52

Knowledge and Necessity   68

''Omne quod est quando est necesse est esse''   72

    Note on Preventing and Producing   82

On Causal Knowledge   86

Diachronic and Synchronic Modality   96

Logical Modality   104

Natural Modality   117

Laws of Nature   134

Subject Index   150

Index of Persons   154

Introduction and Acknowledgements

After the publication of *Explanation and Understanding* in 1971 my main concern in philosophy came to centre round the idea of "determinism". It had been a tenet of that work that determinism in the sphere of natural events and the sphere of human actions differ radically from one another. In two subsequent books, *Causality and Determinism* (1974) and *Freedom and Determination* (1980), I tried to clarify my thoughts on this difference. In the course of these efforts new questions constantly cropped up and many of them were oriented not so much towards the distinction between events and actions as towards the ideas of truth and knowledge and the modal notions of necessity and possibility. Some of the problems, moreover, had notable traditions in Ancient and Medieval philosophy which had been revived in recent thought, particularly by people working in the logico-analytical mainstream of modern philosophy. Examples are the Aristotelian problem of the "Sea Battle", the Diodorean κυριεύων, and the Schoolmen's difficulties in reconciling God's omniscience with human freedom and responsibility. The work of distinguished contemporaries—Anscombe, Hintikka, Prior, and Jules Vuillemin to mention a few—stirred me to efforts of my own in a similar direction. They were given tentative expression in my Nellie Wallace Lectures at Oxford in 1978 on "Some Ancient Problems of Time, Truth, and Necessity" and in a lecture course at the Collège de France called "Truth, Knowledge, and Certainty" two years later. The studies here published under the titles "Determinism and Future Truth", "Determinism and Knowledge of the Future", and "Knowledge and Necessity" got their final form in the Belgum Memorial Lectures which I gave at Saint Olaf College, Northfield, Minnesota in the Autumn 1983. I am grateful for the many opportunities I have had to present my ideas to responsive audiences representing different backgrounds and traditions.

For some time I planned to fuse the work I was doing on truth, knowledge, and modality into the unity of a book. The heterogeneity of the material forced me in the end to abandon the idea. What is presented here is essentially a collection of separate essays. But they have a greater thematic unity than the papers collected in the volumes *Practical Reason* and *Philosophical Logic* and there are frequent cross-references between the individual studies.

In the late 1950s I published a paper on the concept of negation which came to have a seminal influence on my subsequent work in philosophical logic.[1] Its basic idea was a distinction between two forms of negation, a weak and a strong form. "Classical" negation is weak—it signifies, roughly speaking, "nothingness", mere absence of something. Strong negation is related to the notion of a *contrary* rather than to that of a *contradictory*. It stands for the opposite to something "positive"—like privation in relation to possession of a property or forbearance in relation to performance of an action. A similar distinction can be made between "not true" and "false". Falsehood, however, may be defined as truth of the contradictory of a proposition. This opens a possibility of defining strong negation in the more "classical" terms of (weak) negation and truth. The "non-classical" feature of the logic which can then be built is, *not* that it employs an unorthodox kind of negation, but that it incorporates the concept of truth in its object-language as an "operator" on propositions, analogous to the notions of possibility and necessity in modal logic. How this is done I tried to show, for the logic of propositions, in a paper published in a *Festschrift* for Professor Sören Halldén[2] and, for predicate logic, in a *Festschrift* for Professor Oiva Ketonen.[3] Both papers are from the year 1973. They may be regarded as early forms of the essays "Truth and Logic" and "The Logic of Predication" published in this collection.

I believe that truth-logic, or alethic logic as it may also be called, can be used for shedding light on the relation between what may be called logic in the "traditional" sense and another type of logic which, though it too has early roots in the history of thought, is chiefly associated with the name of Hegel and with so-called Dialectical Logic. Efforts are today made in different quarters at a *rapprochement* between these two traditions. It is premature to evaluate their success—and it seems to me best to let the efforts be pursued independently of one another, at least for the time being. This is why, in the two appendices to the paper "Truth and Logic" which deal with questions bordering on dialectical logic, I have not made any reference to related ventures in recent literature. For stimulating discussions on the topics of contradiction and "dialectical synthesis" I am indebted to two young scholars, Antti Hautamäki in Helsinki and Hristo Smolenov in Sofia.

---

[1] "On the Logic of Negation", *Commentationes physico-mathematicae Societatis Scientiarum Fennicae,* **XXII** (4), 1959; available in reprint by University Microfilms International. See also the Introduction to *Philosophical Logic (Philosophical Papers II),* Basil Blackwell, Oxford, 1983.

[2] "Truth as Modality". In *Modality, Morality and Other Problems of Sense and Nonsense.* Essays dedicated to Sören Halldén, Gleerups, Lund, 1973.

[3] "Remarks on the Logic of Predication", *Ajatus,* **35**, 1973.

The essay "Determinism and Future Truth" had two published predecessors which were partly also historical studies on Aristotle. One was called "Determinismus, Wahrheit und Zeitlichkeit, ein Beitrag zum Problem der zukünftigen kontingenten Wahrheiten";[4] the other, which appeared in a *Festschrift* in honour of Elizabeth Anscombe, had the title "Time, Truth, and Necessity".[5]

A preliminary version of "Determinism and Knowledge of the Future" with a postscript on "Knowledge and Necessity" was published in the series of publications of the Finnish Society for Future Research.[6] The essay "On Causal Knowledge" again first appeared in a *Festschrift* for Norman Malcolm and is here republished with the kind permission of the copyright holder.[7]

The comments on the Aristotelian *dictum* "Omne quod est quando est necesse est esse" was in origin a paper for a symposium of the Nordic Plato Society in Copenhagen in 1979. A first version of the paper on diachronic and synchronic modalities was published that same year in the Spanish periodical *Teorema* and a second version some years later in *Acta Philosophica Fennica*.[8] The research embodied in these papers was in origin allied to my efforts to reconstruct the much-debated Master Argument of Diodorus Cronus published in an essay, not included here, in a *Festschrift* for Jaakko Hintikka.[9]

The three concluding studies, on logical and natural modality and on laws of nature, have no predecessors in my earlier literary output.

Georg Henrik von Wright

---

[4] *Studia Leibnitiana*, **6**, 1974.

[5] In *Intention and Intentionality*. Essays in Honour of G.E.M. Anscombe, ed. by Cora Diamond and Jenny Teichman. The Harvester Press, Brighton, 1979.

[6] *Tulevaisuuden Tutkimuksen Seuran Julkaisu A4,* Turku, 1982.

[7] *Knowledge and Mind,* ed. by Carl Ginet and Sydney Shoemaker. Copyright © 1983 by Oxford University Press, Inc.

[8] *Intensional Logic: Theory and Applications,* edited by I. Niiniluoto and E. Saarinen. *Acta Philosophica Fennica,* vol. **35**, 1982.

[9] "The 'Master Argument' of Diodorus". In *Essays in Honour of Jaakko Hintikka,* ed. by E. Saarinen, R. Hilpinen, I. Niiniluoto, and M.B. Provence Hintikka. D. Reidel Publishing Co., Dordrecht, Holland, 1979.

Determinism and Future Truth

I

The ninth chapter of *De Interpretatione* has long puzzled philosophers and logicians. Did Aristotle, or did he not, hold that contingent propositions about the future are (now) either true or false? He would evidently have agreed that it is (now) certain that there will be a sea battle or will not be a sea battle tomorrow, and he realized that from accepting this it does not follow that it is either certain (now) that there will be a sea battle tomorrow or certain (now) that there will not be a sea battle tomorrow. But would he have agreed that one of the two propositions, *viz.* the proposition that there will be a sea battle tomorrow and the proposition that there will not be a sea battle tomorrow, is (now) *true*? On this question interpreters of Aristotle disagree.

More interesting than the question of what was Aristotle's way out of the difficulties which vexed him, I find the question of how the problems themselves which we encounter here have to be solved. I have dealt with this in earlier papers.[1] It has seemed to me that my "way out" would also have had Aristotle's approval. But on this last point I have not been able to rid myself entirely of doubts. In this new attack on the problem I shall altogether disregard the possible opinions of the Stagirite.

II

Consider the following statement:

    (1) It is true that there will be a sea battle tomorrow or there will not be a sea battle tomorrow.

Is this not an indisputably true statement? But, if so, is it then not also indisputably true that

    (2) It is true that there will be a sea battle tomorrow or it is true that there will not be a sea battle tomorrow?

If we admit this distribution of (1) into (2) have we then not thereby implicitly admitted that now the truth of one of the two, mutually ex-

---

[1] See above, Introduction, p. ix.

clusive and jointly exhaustive, alternatives is settled for tomorrow—even though we need not know which one of the two will turn out to be true?

It may thus look as if from accepting (1) we are led, by logical argument, to accept that the truth of everything which will be is predetermined, already settled before it is—in fact at any time beforehand. Because the substance of the above argument would not be changed if for "tomorrow" we substitute a reference to any time, however remote, in the future. Accepting this consequence of (1) and (2) is tantamount to accepting (a form of) *determinism*.

III

Let us next take a closer look at the statements (1) and (2).

Statement (1) I am going to call an application of the Law of Excluded Middle to the proposition that there will be a sea battle tomorrow. By the Law of Excluded Middle I then understand the principle of logic which says that the disjunction of any given proposition and its negation is logically, and therewith also necessarily, true.

Statement (2) is a disjunction. The second disjunct says that it is *true* that there will *not* be a sea battle tomorrow. But this is tantamount to saying that it is *false* that there will be a sea battle tomorrow. Generally speaking: I shall regard it as a *definition* of the predicate "false" that falsehood is the truth of the negation (contradictory) of a proposition. This is not as trivial as it may sound. We must distinguish between the truth of the negation (= falsehood) and the negation of truth, between the phrases "true that not" and "not true that". The importance of this distinction will be discussed in a later chapter.[2]

Accepting the equivalence of meaning between "true that not" and "false that" allows us to transform (2) into

(3) It is true that there will be a sea battle tomorrow or it is false that there will be a sea battle tomorrow.

Allowing this move, statement (2) thus says, implicitly, that the proposition that there will be a sea battle tomorrow is either true or false. The general principle which says that any given proposition is either true or false, i.e. has one of the two truth-values "true" and "false", is known as the Principle or Law of Bivalence. Our statement (2) is then an application of the Law of Bivalence to the particular proposition that there will be a sea battle tomorrow.

The proposition that there will be a sea battle tomorrow exemplifies a

---

[2] See below, especially p. 27f.

future contingency. And similarly its negation, that there will not be a sea battle then. The impression that the application of the Laws of Excluded Middle and of Bivalence to contingent propositions about the future entails a commitment to determinism I shall label an "illusion". The problem with which I am here concerned is how to dispel the illusion. I shall not maintain that what has been said above gives an accurate and exhaustive characterization of the problem which worried Aristotle in the famous ninth chapter. But I think it is difficult to read this chapter without being worried oneself by the problem as here described.[3]

IV

Before presenting my own solution to the puzzle, I shall briefly mention two other proposed ways out of the difficulties. I think neither of them is acceptable; but both contain ideas which deserve to be further discussed.

The first denies the legitimacy of the distributive step from (1) to (2) (or (3)). This solution was suggested by Łukasiewicz to whom, I think, belongs the chief credit for having revived the debate about future contingencies in contemporary philosophical logic.[4]

Łukasiewicz stressed the importance of keeping distinct the two principles which I here, following him, call the Laws of Excluded Middle and of Bivalence respectively. In order to dispel our "deterministic illusion" it is not necessary to reject or restrict the validity of the former, Łukasiewicz notes.[5] But the latter, according to him, is not unrestrictedly valid. It does not, for example, hold good for contingent propositions about the future. Such propositions lack truth-value, are neither true nor false.

Łukasiewicz also makes the following interesting observation:[6] The two disjuncts in the disjunction after the phrase "it is true that" in (1) stand in

---

[3] Opinions differ on the question of what Aristotle's main concern in *De Int. 9* was. See the essay by Jaakko Hintikka: "The once and future sea fight: Aristotle's discussion of future contingents in *De Interpretatione 9*", in his collection of essays *Time and Necessity, Studies in Aristotle's Theory of Modality,* The Clarendon Press, Oxford, 1973, especially pp. 147–53.

[4] Jan Łukasiewicz, "O Determiniźmie", published posthumously in the collection of papers by Łukasiewicz, *Z zagadnieh logiki i filosofii,* ed. by J. Słupecki, Warszawa, 1961. The paper was in origin an address which Łukasiewicz delivered as Rector (Vice-Chancellor) of the University of Warsaw at the inauguration of the academic year 1922–3. There is an English translation by Z. Jordan in *Polish Logic 1920–1939,* ed. by Storrs McCall, Oxford, 1967 and another by Rose Rand in *The Polish Review,* **13,** 1968. A German translation, by Günther Patzig, appeared in *Studia Leibnitiana,* **5,** 1973.

[5] *Op. cit.,* Section 11.

[6] *Op. cit.,* Section 9.

what he calls a contradictory relationship to one another. This is why one may, with Aristotle, assume that (1) is necessarily true. But the two disjuncts which make up (2) do not stand in a contradictory relationship; neither of the two is the negation of the other. Therefore (2) cannot necessarily be true. It may, in fact, be false.

Łukasiewicz's rejection of the Principle of Bivalence for future contingencies was a starting point for his grand conception of a many-valued logic, related to "classical" two-valued logic in a way which is analogous to the relation between non-Euclidean and Euclidean geometry. Łukasiewicz was not the first to entertain the idea of a polyvalent logic. But he gave a decisive impetus to its modern development.

V

The second suggested solution to our problem which I shall reject as unsatisfactory has to do with the semantic status of the phrase "it is true that". This phrase, when prefixed to a sentence which expresses a proposition, is often said to be semantically otiose or redundant or vacuous. The idea is sometimes given the form of an identity:

"it is true that p" = "p"

where the letter "p" might represent, for example, the sentence "there will be a sea battle tomorrow".

It is not clear by itself how we shall understand the identity sign here—whether it designates identity of meaning of the two sentences or identity of truth-value of the propositions which they express. But whether we understand it in one way or the other, the idea seems to imply that the two members of the equation are intersubstitutable *salva veritate* at least in some contexts. Let us assume that our statements (1) and (2) qualify as such contexts. Then (1) reduces to the statement

   (4) There will be a sea battle tomorrow or there will not be a sea battle tomorrow.

But (2), after the substitution, also reduces to this. Thus (1) and (2) both say exactly the same, at least from the point of view of truth, *viz.* that there will be a sea battle tomorrow or there will not be a sea battle tomorrow. And if this is what (1) and (2) both say, the impression that the passage from (1) to (2) involves a commitment to determinism must be an illusion.

Accepting the idea about the vacuous character of the phrase "it is true that", one could also say that any attempt to drive a wedge between the

Law of Excluded Middle and the Law of Bivalence is a vain manoeuvre. With this insight the "deterministic illusion" is dispelled.

This "solution", however, is too cheap to be good. Because, as we shall see later (below, Section XII), it hinges on the assumption that contingent propositions about the future *have* a truth-value. And this is precisely what some people, for example Łukasiewicz, have thought necessary to deny in order not to have to accept the consequence that the truth-value of propositions about the future is predetermined.

VI

Let tomorrow be day *t*. Assume that there is a sea battle on that day. Then it is true that there is a sea battle at *t* (on that day). *When* is this true? Tomorrow? Or "already" today?

Assume that somebody had said yesterday that there will be a sea battle the day after tomorrow. Or, since tomorrow (when writing this) is 14 January 1981, assume that somebody had said on 14 January 1881 that there will be a sea battle somewhere exactly 100 years later—or that somebody in ancient Greece had said that after so and so many sunrises in the place where he was living there would somewhere be a sea battle before sunset in his place. *If* tomorrow there was a sea battle these people were surely *right*. They spoke *the truth*. What they said was *true*. What did they say? They said that there will be a sea battle on 14 January 1981. So was *it* not *true* when they made the statement? But "it" is the proposition that there will be a sea battle tomorrow, i.e. on 14 January 1981.

We are thus led to the following idea: If there is a sea battle on 14 January 1981 the proposition that there is a sea battle then is true at any time before, on, or after the date in question. Or, putting "*p*" for "there is a sea battle" and "at *t*" for "on 14 January 1981": If *p* at *t*, then the proposition that *p* at *t* is always or sempiternally true. But rather than calling its truth "sempiternal", I think we should call it "atemporal" and say that "true at *t*" here simply means "*true*".

I shall refer to this atemporal notion of truth as *plain truth*. When plain truth is in question such locutions as "true today" or "already true" mean nothing over and above "true", and "not yet true" means the same as "not true".

VII

When plain truth is concerned, "is" in "it is true that" is not the tensed "is" which occurs in the combination "is now" or "is already". It is a tenseless "is" like in "twice two is four". The tenseless "is" has no past form "was" or future form "will be". Nor can it be temporally specified as in the phrase "is at *t*".

In spite of this, however, tensed uses of the verb "is" often occur in phrases attributing plain truth to a proposition. I doubt whether we could label such uses "ungrammatical". But they can be replaced by locutions using the tenseless "is" in "it is true that". Some examples will be given to illustrate this:

One might say "it is now true that there is a sea battle" meaning that it is true that there is a sea battle (going on) now or, simply, that a sea battle is now being fought. One might also say "it was true in 1750 that France was a monarchy then". Or, "that France is a monarchy was true in 1750". And this again can be restated in the form "It is true that France was a monarchy in 1750". The future form "it will be true" can also be used in attributions of plain truth, as when we say "it will be true tomorrow that the sky is clearing up" meaning that it is true that the sky will clear up tomorrow.

Generally speaking, when plain truth is in question the schematic phrase "it is (was, will be) true at *t* that ..." can be transformed into the phrase "it is true that at *t* ...", where the eliminated tensed form of the verb "is" is reflected in the tense of the sentence expressing what is said to be true.

VIII

It follows from what has been said, that plain truth is something "unchangeable" or "imperishable". It does not come into being, nor does it cease to be. One could say of it that "once true, always true"—but then one must distinguish the temporal "once" and "always" from an atemporal meaning of these words in that combination.

But do we not speak of things becoming true and ceasing to be true and of things sometimes being true and sometimes not true? Surely we do this—also when the truth under consideration is what I have here called the atemporal notion of plain truth. So how then shall we understand these locutions?

The answer is obtained from a closer inspection of the "things" to which truth is attributed. These things I have already called propositions. Some logicians and philosophers would prefer to call them sentences. This may be done—but in order to explain what it means to attribute truth to a sentence we must, I think, refer to the proposition which the sentence in question expresses, i.e. to *what the sentence says*. Truth, therefore, is *primarily* an attribute of propositions and not of sentences. (On the notion of "proposition" see the next essay.)

With regard to propositions we have to notice here the following distinction. That it is raining is a proposition. But this proposition is not "by itself" true or false. In order to be either it must become associated with a time and a place. That it was raining in Paris on 1 January 1900 is true or false, as the case might have been.

The association with time and space is often implicit in the linguistic context. If I use the sentence "it is raining" for making a statement, I normally mean that it is raining "here and now", i.e. in the place and at the time of my making the statement.

I have elsewhere[7] called the two types of proposition *generic* and *individual*. Generic propositions are a species of what is also called propositional functions. Their truth-value is a function of a spatio-temporal individuation. We can here ignore the spatial component. I shall say that in the schematic phrase "p at t" the letter "p" stands for a sentence expressing a generic proposition such that "p at t" expresses an individual proposition.

For a given "p" the schema "p at t" may turn out to be a true proposition for some value of "t" and a false proposition for some other value. One can then say that the generic proposition that p, for example that it is raining in Paris, is sometimes true and sometimes not. One can also speak of its coming true (at a certain time) and its ceasing to be true. If the schema turns out to be a true proposition for all values of "t" we say that the *generic* proposition that p is *sempiternally* true. For example, the propositions that the earth is shifting its position relative to the sun and that it is rotating round its axis may be thought of as ("practically") sempiternal truths. The sempiternal truth of the generic proposition that the earth is moving must not be confused with the atemporal (and in this sense "eternal" or "sempiternal") truth of the individual proposition that the earth is moving at time t.

Truth, when attributed to generic propositions, is temporal, or better: temporalized; (plain) truth attributed to individual propositions is atemporal. But the meaning of an attribution of (temporalized) truth to a generic proposition is, as we have seen, explicated in terms of an attribution of (atemporal) truth to some individual proposition(s). The former type of attribution is thus secondary to the latter—and the concept of

---

[7] In *Norm and Action, A Logical Inquiry,* Routledge & Kegan Paul, London, 1963, Chapter II, Section 4.

truth involved in both types of attribution is what I have here called "plain truth".

I have dwelt on these distinctions at some length because I think they are important when discussing the idea of truth. A failure to make them clear may have also contributed to confusions in the debates concerning future contingencies.

IX

So far I have been talking about "plain" truth. But not all truth is "plain".

The phrase "it is true" and its tensed variations such as "it was true", "will be true", "is now true", "today true", "already true", "not yet true", when applied to individual propositions, *also* has a use which is genuinely temporal and cannot be reduced to uses of the atemporal notion of plain truth.

For example: "That there will be a sea battle tomorrow is now true; the admirals have just decided that the fleet will fight." Or: "It is already true that there will be an eclipse of the moon on such and such a night in the year 2000; this may be calculated from the laws of planetary motion. That this be true was fixed from the dawn of creation."

It cannot be disputed that these are genuinely temporal uses of the phrase "it is true" and its tensed variations. But one might dispute that they are genuine uses of the word "true". What I mean is the following:

In the examples mentioned one can for the word "true" substitute some other words which express the intended meaning of the sentences at least equally well or maybe with greater clarity. One such word, perhaps the most telling one, is "certain". "It is now certain that there will be a sea battle tomorrow. The admirals have just decided that the fleet is going to fight. But one hour ago this was not yet certain." Other words of a very colloquial character which will also do here are "fixed" or "settled". A more "philosophical" one is the word "necessary". It would suit the second example we gave particularly well: "It is already necessary, and was so from the dawn of creation, that there will be an eclipse of the moon on such and such a night in the year 2000."

It should be observed that the notion of certainty which we encounter here is *not* the epistemic ("subjective") idea of someone being certain of something. It is an ontic or objective certainty which is there independently of whether anybody knows about it.[8] Even if man had never been

---

[8] I must therefore disagree with Moore, when he writes in his paper "Certainty" (*Philosophical Papers*, Allen & Unwin, London, 1959, p. 240) as follows: "It is, indeed, obvious, I think, that a thing can't be certain, unless it is *known*: this is one obvious point that

able to figure out the regularities of planetary motion, it would be certain now that there will be an eclipse on such and such a future day. But this certainty would, of course, not be there if the regularities concerned did not, as a matter of fact, hold good.

When the phrase "it is true that" is used in a genuinely temporal sense, one cannot only substitute for "true" the words "certain" or "necessary". One can also substitute for it a compound "certainly true" or "necessarily true". In the compound we distinguish two components, *viz.* truth and certainty or necessity. The first is "plain" truth and, as such, atemporal. It is the second component which is accountable for the temporal character of the phrase.

Certainty and necessity function here as what I propose to call *diachronic modalities.*[9] An individual proposition which is certain now need not have been this always. The proposition *was* always true in that spurious sense of "always" which really designates atemporality. But it *became* certain—and therefore also true in the compound sense of certainly true.

Similar observations apply to the idea of necessary truth. A man falls from the top of the Eiffel tower and is killed. That his death occurs at time *t* is an atemporal, "eternal" truth. That he should die precisely then was necessary from the moment he fell down. After having fallen over the barrier he was "doomed". But that he fell was, let us assume, accidental. Before he fell it was not necessary that his death was going to occur at time *t*.

When the phrase "it is true that" is used temporally, I say that the use of "true" is not "plain" but *spurious.*[10] But this spurious use, as we have

---

distinguishes the use of the word 'certain' from that of the word 'true'; a thing that nobody knows may quite well be true, but cannot possibly be certain. We can, then, say that it is a necessary condition for the truth of 'It is certain that p' that somebody should know that p is true."—But this cannot be so. Assume that there was an earthquake in a district and that nobody had anticipated it. Afterwards geologists find that, in view of some hitherto unknown facts about the geology of the region, the earthquake *was* in fact, as the experts then would say, *certain* to happen. Must this not be considered an entirely normal and quite common use of "certain"? To suggest that one should say that the earthquake was, in view of those facts, (causally) *necessary*, but *not* say that it was *certain*, would seem to me to be misdirected pedantry.

[9] See the essay "Diachronic and Synchronic Modalities" later in this volume.

[10] A nice example of the spurious use of "true" in philosophic argumentation is provided by the paper by Łukasiewicz mentioned above. If something is the case at time *t* then it is at any later time true that this was the case then, but not (necessarily) at any time before *t*, Łukasiewicz says (*op. cit.*, Section 2). If it had been true "beforehand" that a certain thing was going to be the case at *t* then this thing would of (causal) necessity have had to be (*ibid.*, Section 8.) Somewhat surprisingly, Łukasiewicz also says in one place that "every truth is atemporal" (*ibid.*, Section 2.)

seen, can be debunked as signifying a compound idea of two components. One of the components is "plain" atemporal truth; the other is a diachronic modality of certainty or necessity.

X

We now return to the puzzle about future truth.

The phrase "it is true that" in (1) and (2) above may be given either an atemporal or a temporalized reading, i.e. be understood as referring either to the notion of "plain" truth or to truth which is certain or necessary. Moreover, if the distributive step from (1) to (2) involves a commitment to determinism, it is necessary that the phrase as it occurs in (2) be given the temporalized reading. This is what actually happens when we say, with emphasis, that if the passage from (1) to (2) is logically allowed then either the proposition that there will be a sea battle tomorrow or its negation (contradictory) is true *already now.* If we do not notice the distinction between the two readings of "it is true that" and do not wish to accept this deterministic conclusion, then we must either, as did Łukasiewicz, deny the logical validity of the distributive step from the Law of Excluded Middle to the Law of Bivalence *or,* if we do not question the validity of this step, deny the validity of the Law of Excluded Middle itself for future contingencies.

When the distinction between the two readings is duly noted, the difficulties disappear. "It is certain that there will be a sea battle tomorrow or there will not be a sea battle tomorrow" sounds as acceptable as "it is true that there will be a sea battle tomorrow or there will not be a sea battle tomorrow". But it is also quite obvious that from the former it does not follow that it is certain that there will be a sea battle tomorrow or it is certain that there will not be a sea battle tomorrow. The same observations hold good if for "certain" we put "fixed", "settled", or "necessary". None of these words can be distributed in the same way as the word "true" *when plain truth is concerned.*

One could also express these insights as follows: The principle which we have called the Law of Excluded Middle has the same degree of plausibility for plain truth as for necessary truth and certainty. But with the principle we have called the Law of Bivalence things stand differently. When plain truth is concerned it seems just as acceptable as the Law of Excluded Middle, and the distributive step from the one to the other seems unproblematic. But when the notion of necessary truth is concerned it seems much less obvious than the Law of Excluded Middle and the distributive step is quite clearly logically invalid. The same observation holds for certainty.

Thus the wedge which Łukasiewicz and some other logicians have wanted to drive between the two laws certainly *is* there when the type of truth under consideration is certain or necessary truth. To remove the wedge would be to lapse into determinism. But its removal would also be contrary to sound logical reasoning. What I have called the "illusion of determinism" has one of its roots in a tacit oscillation or shift in the understanding from an atemporal reading of the phrase "it is true that" to a temporalized reading of it. A crucial step in the argument which seems legitimate and uncontroversial under the first reading is quite obviously not allowed under the second reading.

Nothing which has been said here in order to dispel the illusion amounts to a denial or a proposed refutation of determinism. Maybe it *is* already today settled whether there will be a sea battle tomorrow or not—only we do not know "which way" this has been settled. Maybe it was settled even "from the dawn of creation". Surely there are *some* propositions about future events, the truth of which *is* certain or necessary in advance—such as, for example, forecasts of eclipses of the moon or the sun. What is, at best, controversial is whether this holds good for *all* propositions and whether it ever, for any proposition, does this "from the dawn of creation".

XI

In order to solve the puzzle about future contingent truth it is thus not only not necessary to deny the validity of the Law of Excluded Middle. It is also not necessary to doubt its equivalence with the Law of Bivalence when "plain truth" is concerned. I hope that I have been able to show this convincingly. Two things, however, I have *not* shown. One is that the two laws actually *are* equivalent for the notion of truth (I shall henceforth drop the adjective "plain"). The other is that these principles are true (valid).

I shall not here discuss these questions. In another essay ("Truth and Logic", below p. 26ff.), I shall try to show, on the one hand, that the two laws of logic are equivalent, but that, on the other hand, neither of them is unrestrictedly valid for all propositions whatsoever.

Before concluding the present paper, I shall return to a point which was already touched upon in the previous discussion (Section V). It concerns the supposedly otious or vacuous character of the phrase "it is true that". Some people, including myself in past writings, have thought that there is a short cut to the solution of the puzzles relating to future contingent truth based upon an assumed equivalence of the two schemata "it is true that *p*" and "*p*" when "*p*" stands for a sentence which expresses a proposition. The reason why I think this proposal no good for solving the puzzles is that it begs the question of truth-value. I shall now elaborate my objection to it in some detail.

XII

As already indicated in Section V, it is not entirely clear what the purported equivalence or, as it is sometimes also called, "identity" of the two schemata amounts to. But if it is to serve as a short cut to a solution of the problem about future contingencies it must, at least, amount to intersubstitutability *salva veritate* (in the relevant contexts). If this condition is to be satisfied, the two schemata must, when instantiated, necessarily yield propositions with the same truth-value. This means the following:

If it is true that it is true that *p,* then it is also true that *p,* and vice-versa. And if it is false that it is true that *p,* then it is false that *p,* and vice-versa.

There are thus four relations of implication involved. Do they all hold good? We pick out for consideration the one which may seem least obviously true, and ask: Is it necessarily the case that if it is false that it is true that *p,* then it is false that *p*?

Assume that the proposition that *p* lacked truth-value, i.e. were neither true nor false. Then, obviously, it would be false to say that it is true that *p.* But it would not follow that it is false that *p*—since this proposition is neither true nor false. Or, to put the point about "not follow" a little differently: It would then be true that it is false that it is true that *p*—but it would not be true that it is false that *p.* Therefore the second does not follow from the first. Because that something follows from something else must here mean that if the second is true, the first is also true. And this is not now the case.

Thus at least one of the four implications is not logically valid. Therefore the two schemata "it is true that *p*" and "*p*" cannot be equivalent in the sense of being intersubstitutable *salva veritate* either.

My counterargument hinges upon the assumption that the proposition that *p* is neither true nor false. But is this not a queer assumption to make? *Are* not all propositions either true or false—"by definition" somebody may even wish to say?

This question must still be discussed. Be it observed, however, that if the schema

"it is true that *p*" = "*p*"

is valid for all propositions whatsoever then it follows from (1) above that it is either true that there will be, or true that there will not be, a sea battle tomorrow. It can indeed be disputed that this involves a commitment to determinism. But in order to dispel successfully what I called "the deterministic illusion" here we must not (tacitly) take for granted the very thing which some of the disputants think necessary to reject. The trick then begs the question.

Demystifying Propositions

I

In the essay on future truth I used the term "proposition" and said that sentences may be pronounced true or false only via the propositions which they express (above, p. 6f.).

Truth and falsity are commonly and naturally predicated of beliefs and judgements. Also of statements and, maybe, assertions—although, I must confess, it slightly offends my "logical ear" to hear assertions pronounced true or false. And to say this of sentences seems to me definitely barbaric. I have this impression independently of whether sentences are conceived of as types or as tokens.

It is noteworthy, however, that the "logic" built into different languages differs here. I suppose that the German "*Satz*" is as adequate a translation of the English "sentence" as one might wish for. But to say of a *Satz* in German that it is true or false does not offend the ear. To translate into German a philosophic text in English, the author of which has carefully observed the sentence–proposition distinction, can therefore be connected with difficulties. Similarly it is sometimes awkward to render *Satz* in a German text consistently as "sentence" in English—as, for example, translators of Wittgenstein must have experienced.

Talk of true or false *propositions*, using that term, can hardly be said to be part and parcel of colloquial English. "Proposition" as a technical term of philosophical logic sounds like a philosopher's invention. I do not know the history of the term. Its use is characteristic of a Cambridge tradition in philosophy, chiefly associated with the names of C. D. Broad, W. E. Johnson, G. E. Moore, and Bertrand Russell.

The ordinary way of speaking about truth which most closely parallels or corresponds to the philosopher's talk about propositions is when we say that it is true, or false, *that* so and so (is the case). This, somehow, seems the most basic or direct attribution of truth-value which there is. That certain things are ("objectively") true, others not, is what "makes" beliefs, judgements, statements true or false. The truth-value of these latter is, in a certain way, derivative or secondary. Primarily, truth and falsity belongs to the *content* of beliefs, judgements, and statements, i.e. to *that which* is believed, judged, or stated, and therewith also to that which sentences *say* or *mean* or *express*.

It is for speaking about those "that which"-things that philosophers may find it useful to employ the term "proposition".

But use of this term is apt to engender lots of philosophical mist. Once one has the noun one also gets the idea of some entity or substance. What *are* propositions? What form of being or existence do they partake in? How are they related, on the one hand, to the objective features of reality and, on the other hand, to the phenomena of belief, judgement, and statement which are tied to persons or subjects? What, in particular, is their relationship to language?

II

The bewilderment caused by the notion of "proposition" is amply reflected in the writings of the Cambridge philosophers just mentioned from the first half of this century. In his early work *The Principles of Mathematics*, Russell ventured to *define* the notion as follows. A proposition, he says there,[1] is anything which implies itself. "Hence to say 'p is a proposition' is equivalent to saying 'p implies p'; and this equivalence may be used to define propositions." Implication is indefinable.[2] But "the assertion that q is true or p false turns out to be strictly equivalent to 'p implies q'".[3] From this it follows that to say that p is a proposition is equivalent to saying that p is true or p is false. "By definition" therefore a proposition, on Russell's view here, is either true or false, has a truth-value.

The above quotations from Russell will give rise to some questions. "p" and "q" are *letters*. "p is a proposition" is not meant to say that the letter p is a proposition. The letter is a variable, a schematic representation for something which is asserted to be a proposition. What can we substitute for "p" so as to obtain an example? A *sentence*? A sentence would be, for example, "it is raining". "it is raining is a proposition" does not sound even grammatically correct. If instead of the sentence we substitute a *name* of the sentence and use the familiar device of forming the name of a sentence by enclosing it in quotes, we get "'it is raining' is a proposition". This is grammatically in order. What it says is that a certain sentence is a proposition. "Proposition" would then name a kind of sentence—perhaps any sentence in the indicative mood.

In *Principia Mathematica* Russell distinguished between propositions

---

[1] *The Principles of Mathematics*, Allen & Unwin, London, 1903, p. 15.
[2] *Ibid.*, p. 14.
[3] *Ibid.*, p. 15.

"considered factually" and "considered as vehicles of truth and falsehood".[4] Considered factually, propositions are "classes of similar occurrences"; considered as vehicles of truth and falsehood, they are "particular occurrences".[5] Occurrences of what? the reader may ask. The answer is: of *sentences*.[6] Russell is here referring to the well-known distinction between *type* and *token* of a linguistic expression.

Both in *Principles* and in *Principia*, Russell thus regarded propositions as a kind of "linguistic entity", as a "form of words". And in *Introduction to Mathematical Philosophy* he said expressly: 'We mean by a "proposition" primarily a form of words which expresses what is either true or false.'[7] But in a paper[8] from the very same year as *Introduction* he somewhat modified his position. He now distinguished between "word-propositions" and "image-propositions". A word-proposition *refers* to the objective fact which makes it true or false and *means* a corresponding image-proposition.[9] This presumably echoes a distinction familiar from Frege which has later come to play an important role in philosophical semantics and the philosophy of language generally.

We may note here, on the one hand, a tendency to view propositions as "linguistic entities" and, on the other hand, a reluctance to identify them with merely "a form of words". The same tension is reflected already in the well-known textbook on formal logic by J.N. Keynes.[10] Here it is said: "So far as we treat of propositions in logic, we treat of them not as grammatical sentences, but as assertions, as verbal expressions of judgements".[11] But is not a verbal expression a "mere" form of words then?

The question of how propositions are related to language was also of great concern to W.E. Johnson.[12] His opinions on the matter seem to have vacillated considerably.[13] But at least in his only major work *Logic* he is

---

[4] A. N. Whitehead and Bertrand Russell, *Principia Mathematica*, Cambridge University Press, 1910; 2nd edn, 1925, Volume I, p. 664.

[5] *Ibid.*, p. 665.

[6] *Ibid.*

[7] *Introduction to Mathematical Philosophy*, Allen & Unwin, London, 1919, p. 155.

[8] "On Propositions: what they are and how they mean", *Proceedings of the Aristotelian Society*, Supplementary Volume II, 1919. Here quoted from the collection of essays by Russell, *Logic and Knowledge, Essays 1901–1950*, ed. by R. Ch. Marsh, Macmillan, New York, 1956.

[9] *Logic and Knowledge*, pp. 308–9.

[10] J.N. Keynes, *Formal Logic*, 4th edn., London, 1906.

[11] *Op. cit.,* p. 66.

[12] W.E. Johnson, *Logic*, Part I, Cambridge University Press, Cambridge, 1921.

[13] Cf. the statement by C.D. Broad in *Examination of McTaggart's Philosophy*, Volume I, Cambridge University Press, Cambridge, 1933, p. 69f.

anxious to separate propositions from their counterparts in language. "It has been very generally held", he says,[14] that the proposition is the *verbal expression* of the judgment; this, however, seems to be an error, because such characterizations as true or false cannot be predicated of a mere verbal expression, for which appropriate adjectives would be 'obscure', 'ungrammatical', 'ambiguous', etc.". Johnson then makes a distinction between propositions "subjectively regarded" and "objectively regarded". When viewed under the first aspect a proposition is, he says, an *assertible*; when viewed under the second aspect it is a *possibile*.[15]

G.E. Moore always strictly observed the distinction between proposition and sentence. In the chapter "Propositions" in the early lectures published under the title *Some Main Problems of Philosophy*, Moore wrote: "Whenever I speak of a proposition, I shall always be speaking, *not* of a mere sentence—a mere collection of words, but of what these words *mean*."[16] The term "proposition", he says there, "is a name for what is *expressed* by certain forms of words—those, namely, which, in grammar, are called 'sentences'. It is a name for what is before your mind, when you do not only hear or read but *understand* a sentence. It is, in short, the *meaning* of a sentence—what is expressed or conveyed by a sentence: and is, therefore, utterly different from the sentence itself—from the mere words."[17]

In Moore's view, "To say that an expression is true is simply to say that it expresses a true proposition."[18] In partial agreement with the opinion Russell had expressed in *Principia* (cf. above p. 16) on how truth is related to the type–token distinction, Moore in lectures from the 1920s makes the following good observation: "It is primarily *token-expressions* which are 'true' in this sense: with regard to *type-expressions* to say that it was 'true' would be to say that *every* token-expression which was an instance of it was true, and this is a thing which it would be rash to affirm was ever the case."[19]

In the lectures, Moore thus admitted that there *also* is a sense, albeit a secondary one, in which sentences can be true or false, *viz.* when they express true propositions. "We certainly do say that sentences—mere form of words—are true", he says. But in a footnote from the year 1952

---

[14] *Logic*, I, p. 1.
[15] *Logic*, I, p. 14.
[16] G.E. Moore, *Some Main Problems of Philosophy*, Allen & Unwin, London, 1953, p. 57.
[17] *Ibid.*, p. 259.
[18] G. E. Moore, *Lectures on Philosophy*, ed. by C. Lewy, Allen & Unwin, London, 1966, p. 57.
[19] *Ibid.*, p. 142f.

when the lectures were edited for publication, he added: "I see no reason now to think that we ever do call sentences or forms of words 'true' except in such archaic-sounding expression as 'A true word is often spoken in jest'".[20] It was this taste which I myself acquired in the numerous discussions which I had with Moore during my Cambridge years in the late 1940s and early 1950s.

III

The Cambridge philosophers may be said to have agreed that truth and falsity "primarily" or "properly" belong to propositions.[21] But on the nature of propositions they, as we have seen, held no very clear and still less unanimous opinion.

A question which, as far as I know, none of these philosophers seriously considered was whether a proposition *must* have a truth-value or whether there can be propositions which are neither true nor false.

Moore noted, in passing, that not all *sentences* express propositions. He said he "is not sure" whether "an imperative, such as 'Go away', expresses a proposition at all".[22] The reason for his hesitation was, presumably, that not all sentences express something which is either true or false.

From the "definition" of the concept of a proposition which Russell gave in the *Principles* (see above p. 15) it seemed to follow that propositions have to be either true or false. Because the Russellian relation of implication can hardly be thought to hold between entities void of truth-value. But in the *Principia* Russell divides propositions into *significant* and *non-significant* ones. "Significant", he says,[23] means "either true or false". Russell may thus here be said to have introduced a *trichotomy* "true−false−neither true nor false" in place of the traditional *dichotomy* "true−false" when speaking about truth and propositions. Russell only rarely uses the term "meaningless" which later became current with the logical positivists and was used by them in a sense corresponding, roughly, to that which Russell called "non-significant".

---

[20] *Some Main Problems of Philosophy*, p. 262.

[21] Moore, *Some Main Problems*, p. 63: "Propositions are, then, a sort of thing which may be properly said to be true or false." F.P. Ramsey, "Facts and Propositions" (in *The Foundations of Mathematics*, ed. by R.B. Braithwaite, Kegan Paul, London, 1931), p. 142: "Truth and falsity are ascribed primarily to propositions." C.D. Broad, *Examination of McTaggart's Philosophy*, Volume I, p. 64: "Truth and falsity, in their primary sense, attach to propositions."

[22] *Some Main Problems*, p. 61.

[23] *Principia*, Volume I, p. 45.

As we have seen above (pp. 15f.), Russell was, on the whole, of the opinion that propositions are linguistic entities or (even) "forms of words". In his article on Russell's logic in the Schilpp volume, Reichenbach hails the Russellian trichotomy as "one of the deepest and soundest discoveries of modern logic".[24] It was Russell's great merit, Reichenbach says, to have realized "that the division of linguistic expressions into true and false is not sufficient; that a third category must be introduced with includes *meaningless* expressions."[25]

But if, as Moore was anxious to point out, truth and falsehood are not (directly) attributes of "forms of words" and if propositions, as he said, are the meanings of (certain) sentences, then the talk of meaningful and meaningless *propositions* would itself be nonsense.[26] The two pairs "true–false" and "meaningful–meaningless" are then simply not distinctions on the same logical level of discourse. Both distinctions are important; and that Russell's work greatly contributed to making the conditions of meaningfulness a major problem in modern philosophical logic and logical semantics is undeniable.

Thus we must conclude that the replacement of the dichotomy "true–false" with the trichotomy "true–false–meaningless" does not answer the question whether propositions, when conceived of as the *contents* of beliefs, judgements or statements, and *not* as *linguistic expressions,* must be either true or false or may be void of truth-value altogether.

I shall now turn to this question. But before I answer it, I must venture an opinion of my own on the troublesome entities called "propositions".

IV

Even though I do not think it right to call propositions "linguistic entities" I think that in order to clarify ("demystify") the notion we must start from considerations about language.

I shall here regard as basic the linguistic notion of a well-formed or grammatically correct *sentence* (of a given language). This notion I shall not attempt to clarify or define. One may relegate the task to grammarians and linguists—without thereby implying that the notion itself of a sentence is "philosophically unproblematic".

---

[24] Hans Reichenbach, "Bertrand Russell's Logic", in *The Philosophy of Bertrand Russell*, ed. by P.A. Schilpp, Tudor Publishing Company, New York, 1944, p. 37.

[25] *Ibid.*

[26] It may be noted that Gödel in his paper "Russell's Mathematical Logic" in the Schilpp volume does not hesitate to speak about "meaningful propositions" (p. 149).

Not all well-formed sentences express something which may be associated with a truth-value. For example, an imperative sentence like "Open the window!", or an optative one like "May he come today" or an interrogative one like "What is your name?" do not do this. Aristotle mentions[27] prayers as examples of sentences which say neither the true nor the false.

"What a handsome face!". Is this a sentence? Not, if a sentence must contain a verb. Here the notion of sentence itself begins to waver.

No philosopher would feel tempted to say that sentences such as those mentioned above constitute exceptions to the Law of Bivalence or that they express propositions which lack truth-value. The obvious thing to say is that they do not express propositions at all.[28] In saying this, one would implicitly ask on what conditions a grammatically correct sentence expresses a proposition.

One possible answer is that a sentence expresses a proposition only on condition that it says something which is either true or false.[29] Truth-value would then "by definition" belong to propositions. But there is also another possibility to be considered.

If to the sentences mentioned above we prefix the phrase "it is true that" we do not get a new well-formed sentence of the language. "It is true that open the window" is ungrammatical and *therefore* "meaningless". So are, "it is true that may he come today" and "it is true that what is your name".

If prefixing the phrase "it is true that" to a well-formed sentence *s* yields another well-formed sentence of the language, then I shall say that the sentence *s expresses a proposition* and speak of *the proposition expressed by s*. Since the iteration of the phrase does not change the well-formed character of the sentence, it follows from our definition that also the sentence "it is true that *s*" expresses a proposition. ("It is true that it is true that *s*" is well-formed if "it is true that *s*" is well-formed.)

A sentence *s* with the above properties is usually what grammarians would call an *indicative* sentence. But sentences other than those in the

---

[27] *De Interpretatione*, Chapter IV, 17a4–6.

[28] Cf. the quotation from Moore above, p. 18, fn. 22.

[29] Aristotle, *loc. cit.*, 17a1–4 Ἔστι δὲ λόγος ἅπας μὲν σημαντικός ... ἀποφαντικὸς δὲ οὐ πᾶς, ἀλλ᾿ ἐν ᾧ τὸ ἀληθεύειν ἢ ψεύδεσθαι ὑπάρχει. In the Loeb translation: "But while every sentence has meaning ... not all can be called propositions. We call propositions those only that have truth or falsity in them." Also the translation by E.M. Edghill in the Ross edition of Aristotle's work renders ἀποφαντικὸς by "proposition". This seems to me awkward also on independent philological grounds. A better translation of the term would be "statement". This is used in the new translation by J.L. Ackrill *Aristotle's "Categories" and "De Interpretatione"*, Clarendon Press, Oxford, 1963.

indicative mood can also satisfy our condition for expressing a proposition. An example would be a conditional sentence such as "if he were with us, we might be saved". Its grammatical mood is not indicative. As a common name for proposition-expressing sentences I shall use the term *constative* or *declarative* (sentence). Whether this is a "grammatical" category or not is arguable. But this question need not occupy us here.

V

According to the criterion which we gave, "you must not open the window" is a sentence expressing a proposition. "It is true that you must not open the window" is grammatically well formed. But now: cannot "you must not open the window" be used, on occasions, to mean exactly the same as "don't open the window"? Obviously it can. Must we then say that the second expresses a proposition if we say that the first does?

Here we must not let the notion of a proposition mystify us. When speaking about that which declarative sentences "express", "mean" or "say" we use a linguistic device which consists in prefixing the word "that" to the sentence. We thereby transform the sentence into a *that*-clause, into something which is not itself a *sentence*. Thus we say that it is, not only true or not true, but also possible or obvious or well-known, etc. *that* so and so—the place of "so and so" in the schema being taken by the declarative sentence. Calling that which we are then talking about a "proposition", or saying that the sentence in question "expresses a proposition", is tantamount to saying that to turn the sentence into a that-clause is a *grammatically admissible move in our language*. If we say that the sentence "don't open the window" does not express a proposition what this means is therefore simply that the move from it to "that don't open the window" is grammatically inadmissible.

But if the two sentences can be used for giving the same order (prohibition), do they not, when thus used, "mean" the same? If they mean the same do they not then both express the same proposition? One *could* say this—but then one must be aware that "mean the same" and "express the same proposition" here *means* that the two sentences, although they belong to different grammatical categories of sentence, may both be used for giving the same order.

I hope that what has been said will help to demystify the notion of a proposition. It should also demystify the idea of a proposition without truth-value. A prohibition stated with the words "the window must not be opened" or a permission "you may park your car here" is neither true nor false. But the form of words "it is true that the window must not be opened" and "it is true that you may park your car here" are grammatically correct. These two facts jointly may be "contracted" into saying that the propositions expressed by the two sentences, when used for giving an order or permission respectively, lack truth-value, are neither true nor false.[30]

One could dispense with the term "proposition" entirely and say everything which is said with its aid talking only about grammatically well-formed sentences, that-clauses, and truth-values. Since the term is apt to create confusion and pseudo-problems, it may even be advisable to dispense with it. As a terminological (linguistic) device it is nevertheless useful and I shall continue to employ it now that, at least in principle, we need not let ourselves be mystified by it any more. But I shall avoid such locutions as calling propositions the *reference* of *that*-clauses or the *meanings* of sentences because these locutions are unnecessary and induce us to talk of propositions as of some *entities* with a shadow of existence.

VI

To say that some propositions lack truth-value, are neither true nor false, thus means, on the ruling which we have adopted, that some (tokens of some) grammatically correct sentences of the form "it is true that *s*" (where "*s*" is itself a grammatically correct sentence) say something which is neither true nor false.

We are already familiar with examples. Sentences such as "you ought to open the window" or "one must not smoke in this room", when used for giving prescriptions (orders, norms, rules), do not say anything which is true or false. According to many philosophers, evaluative sentences, such as e.g. "it is better to suffer evil than to do evil" belong in the same

---

[30] "The two sentences" here means instances or tokens of the two sentence-types or of what Russell (see above p. 16) called "classes of similar occurrences". Tokens of the types are sometimes used *prescriptively*, sometimes *descriptively*. When used prescriptively they order or permit something; when used descriptively they state that something has been ordered or permitted. In the second case only do the sentences mean or say something which is either true or false.

It would be a mistake to think that the use of the phrase "it is true that" would, "by itself", serve to distinguish the two cases. Consider the following dialogue: "You may park your car here." "True?" "Yes, yes, it is true that you may park your car here." Adding the phrase "it is true that" does not make the sentence-token express a true or false proposition. Whether it does this or not depends upon whether I use it—with or without the addition of "it is true that"—for giving permission (myself) or for informing my interlocutor that parking has been permitted (by the authorities) in this area.

category. Philosophers of the logical positivist orientation of the mid-century sometimes called such sentences "meaningless".

"Meaningless" in a more substantial sense are sentences which, although correctly formed of familiar words and declarative in form have no use in our language because of lack of criteria for pronouncing them (what they say) true or false. Consider, for example, the sentences "prime numbers are green" or "courage is round". Do we understand these sentences? Yes and no. We understand that the first attributes a certain colour to certain numbers, but we cannot "make sense" of the attribution. One is here almost tempted to say that the meaninglessness of the sentence is shown by its meaning![31] The meaninglessness is *not* a matter of grammatical correctness—like that of the sentence "Socrates is identical". It is not exactly a matter of logical correctness either. The lack of "meaning", as already indicated, is due to the lack of truth-criteria. We could invent such criteria, for example give some rule for associating colours with numbers—and then it might be of interest ("make sense") to find out whether prime numbers have this colour or that one. The sentence that such numbers are green would no longer be meaningless; and similarly for traits of character and geometrical shapes.

A different kind of example is provided by sentences which, seemingly, have a clear meaning but the truth-value of which, for reasons of a logical nature, cannot be decided or established. Consider, for example, the statement that the relative frequency with which a certain characteristic occurs in the members of a potentially infinite extensional sequence such as, say, throws with a coin or a dice, approaches as a limit a given value. As is well known from the philosophy of probability, such a limiting frequency statement cannot be conclusively verified or falsified. But is it not nevertheless true or false? Some would perhaps say that it is, although one cannot decide which truth-value it has. Since, however, the impossibility of coming to know its truth-value is not due to any shortcoming of our epistemic faculties, but to the fact that there *is* no state of affairs corresponding ("objectively") to its truth or falsehood, it is a feasible thing to say here that the proposition asserted with the statement actually is one which *has* no truth-value. Some logical positivists of the 1920s and 1930s would have labelled also such statements "meaningless".

The logical positivists were also worried about unrestricted universal and existential propositions. The first cannot be conclusively verified in extension, i.e. on the basis of facts of experience; the second again cannot be conclusively falsified. Hence one may say that there is no state of

---

[31] This was how G. E. Moore once expressed himself in a conversation with me.

affairs (fact) answering to the truth of the first or to the falsehood of the second. It may be difficult to defend the view that unrestricted universal or existential generalizations are not "genuine" propositions if by "proposition" one means something which is either true or false. Yet it is not unproblematic to say that they are such. (I shall return to this problem later; see below, pp.107ff.)

VII

We have already (p. 7) encountered the distinction between *generic* and *individual* propositions. This distinction has a bearing on the question of associating truth-values with propositions.

Consider the proposition that it is raining. Is it true or false? One could answer: the proposition is either true or false *of* any given place and time—but unless a place and a time is specified its truth-value is indeterminate. It is not, "by itself", true or false. It is true of some places at some times and false of some places at some other times. Its truth-value can thus also be said to *vary* with variations in the spatio-temporal determination.

The needed determination is often supplied by the context of a statement. If I make the statement that it is raining without saying where and when I should normally mean that it is raining then in the place where I happen to be. If, however, I am speaking about remote places or times, I ought usually to supply the spatio-temporal coordinates in language. When this is done, the sentence-token used in making the statement expresses a univocally true or false individual proposition.

Sentences which are well-formed and admit the prefix "it is true that" but which need *a linguistic supplementation* in order univocally to express a proposition with a truth-value, I shall in conformity with received terminology call *open* sentences. When the appropriate linguistic supplementation is made, they become *closed*. Thus the sentences "it is raining" and also "it is true that it is raining" are open; the sentences "it is raining in Paris on 12 November 1980" and "it is true that it is raining in Paris on 12 November 1980" are closed.

Consider the sentence "it is green". It is grammatically well-formed. So also is "it is true that it is green". But unless it is made clear what the "it" refers to, we cannot tell whether the sentence expresses a true or a false proposition or, maybe, a proposition without truth-value. The reference of the word "it" may be clear from the context or it may be indicated in language by a name or a definite description which can take its place. "The dome of the Pantheon in Paris is green" expresses a true proposition; "the number 7 is green" presumably expresses a proposition which is neither true nor false.

The open sentence "it is green" may be said to express a generic proposition with a variable truth-value. Since the linguistic supplementation here needed to close the sentence consists in replacing the word "it" by a name or descriptive phrase, this *word* is also said to be a variable. In books on logic one usually employs letters, say *x*, to indicate such variables or open places in a sentence. If the variable is replaced by the name of some thing and the sentence thus obtained expresses a true individual proposition, we may say that the generic proposition is true *of* that thing.

One could of course say that the generic propositions which open sentences express have no truth-value, are neither true nor false. But the way in which they lack truth-value is quite different from the way in which some other propositions may be said to do this. Generic propositions are not *by themselves* true or false. They are, in a characteristic sense, "incomplete" or "unsaturated". They have a "gap" in themselves which, when filled, may turn them into true or false (individual) propositions. This is why I prefer to say that they have an *indeterminate* or *variable* truth-value rather than saying that they *lack* truth-value.

VIII

Assume that the proposition expressed by "*s*" is neither true nor false. What then about the proposition expressed by the sentence "it is true that *s*"? This proposition *has* a truth-value. It is false, i.e. its negation is true. Because if it is neither true nor false that *s*, then it is obviously false to say that it is true that *s*—or, which is merely a verbal transformation, true to say that it is not true that *s*. This idea is fundamental to the "Logic of Truth" which I am going to construct next. It is therefore important that it be clearly grasped. The idea is that the attribution of truth-value to a proposition which lacks truth-value yields a proposition which is *false*—and not a proposition which is itself void of truth-value.

Truth and Logic

I

I shall construct a calculus which I propose to call the Logic of Truth or Truth-Logic or, for short, TL. An alternative name would be Alethic Logic, from the Greek word for truth, ἀλήθεια. Its basic vocabulary consists of the following ingredients:

(1) Variables $p, q, \ldots$, standing for declarative sentences, i.e. sentences which allow their transformation in language into a *that*-clause (see above, p. 21.)

(2) Two sentential connectives— $\sim$ for negation, corresponding to the word "not" of natural language, and & for conjunction, corresponding to the word "and".

(3) An operator T which reads "it is true that".

(4) Brackets.

By definition, three more sentential connectives are introduced, *viz.* $\vee$, $\rightarrow$, and $\leftrightarrow$. They correspond, *roughly*, to the words "or", "if ... then", and "if, and only if, ... then" of ordinary language. But their precise meanings are given by their definition in the terms of negation and conjunction: $s \vee s' =_{df} \sim (\sim s \& \sim s')$, $s \rightarrow s' =_{df} \sim (s \& \sim s')$ and $s \leftrightarrow s' =_{df} \sim (s \& \sim s') \& \sim (\sim s \& s')$, where s and s' are metavariables representing arbitrary sentences of the calculus.

II

The well-formed expressions or formulas of the calculus will be called T-sentences (-expressions, -formulas). They are either atomic or molecular.

An atomic T-sentence consists of the operator T followed by a variable *or* by a molecular compound of variables *or* by an atomic T-sentence *or* by a molecular compound of atomic T-sentences *or*, finally, by a variable or molecular compound of variables and atomic T-sentences. Thus, for example, Tp is an atomic T-sentence, and so is also $T(p \vee q)$ and $TT \sim p$ and $T(\sim Tp \& T(q \rightarrow r))$ and $T(p \rightarrow Tp)$.

A molecular T-sentence is a molecular compound of atomic T-sentences. For example: $Tp \rightarrow T \sim Tp$.

The conventions for bracketing expressions and for omitting brackets I shall not explain here. I shall regard them as being either known or self-explanatory.

III

The "bases" of the calculus are the following five axioms:

A1. $T \sim p \rightarrow \sim Tp.$
A2. $Tp \leftrightarrow T \sim \sim p.$
A3. $T(p \,\&\, q) \leftrightarrow Tp \,\&\, Tq.$
A4. $T \sim (p \,\&\, q) \leftrightarrow T \sim p \lor T \sim q.$
A5. $T \sim Tp \leftrightarrow \sim Tp.$

Falsehood may be defined as the truth of the negation (contradictory) of a proposition (cf. above, p. 2). What the five axioms say can then be stated in words as follows:

A1 says that a false proposition is not true. A2 says that a proposition is true if, and only if, its negation is false. A3 says that the conjunction of two propositions is true if, and only if, both conjuncts are true. A4 says that a conjunction of two propositions is false if, and only if, at least one of the conjuncts is false. A5, finally, says that it is false that a proposition is true if, and only if, the proposition in question is not true.

If in A4 we substitute "$\sim p$" and "$\sim q$" for "p" and "q" and apply to the left membrum of the equivalence the definition of disjunction and simplify the right membrum by virtue of A2, we obtain the formula $T(p \lor q) \leftrightarrow Tp \lor Tq.$ This may be regarded as an alternative form of A4.[1]

The most interesting, and perhaps controversial, axiom is A5. In order to see what is interesting about it, consider a proposition to which we do not wish to accord truth-value, for example, that prime numbers are green. Then it is not true that prime numbers are green. Nor is it false.

---

[1] There is also another, more restrictive, way of laying down the truth-condition for disjunction. One would then say that a disjunction of two propositions is true if, and only if, both disjuncts are true or one is true and the other false. This is equivalent with saying that a conjunction is false if, and only if, both conjuncts are false or one is false and the other true. On this more restrictive conception, A3 and A4 together specify the truth-conditions for a conjunction (disjunction) in such a way that, if one conjunct (disjunct) happens to be neither true nor false, then the conjunction (disjunction) is void of truth-value, too. The choice between the two conceptions of the truth-conditions seems to me very much a matter or arbitrary convention. I have previously myself favoured the more restrictive view. A4 is then given the form $T \sim (p \,\&\, q) \leftrightarrow T \sim p \,\&\, T \sim q \lor Tp \,\&\, T \sim q \lor T \sim p \,\&\, Tq.$ Cf. my paper "Truth as Modality" in *Modality, Morality and Other Problems of Sense and Nonsense*, Essays dedicated to Sören Halldén, Gleerup, Lund, 1973.

This being so, it is *true* that it is not true that prime numbers are green and, since "true that not" means "false", it is *false* that it is true that prime numbers are green. What A5 says, in effect, is that although there may exist propositions which are neither true nor false, any (declarative) sentence beginning "it is true that" expresses a proposition which *is* either true or false (cf. above p. 12 and p. 25).

IV

The class of theorems of our Logic of Truth or *T*-Logic is defined as follows:

(1) A *T*-formula which is a substitution instance of a tautology of "classical" Propositional Logic (PL) is a theorem of TL. A substitution instance is that which we get when we replace all variables in a tautology of PL by *T*-formulas. For example: $p \lor \sim p$ is a tautology of PL, hence $Tp \lor \sim Tp$ is a theorem of TL.

(2) The axioms A1–A5 of TL are theorems.

(3) Theorems, finally, are all *T*-formulas which can be obtained from theorems of TL with the aid of one or several of the following rules of transformation:

R1. Substitution, i.e. the replacement of variables $p, q, \ldots$ by other variables or by molecular compounds of variables or by *T*-formulas. For example: since $Tp \lor \sim Tp$ is a theorem, $T \sim Tp \lor \sim T \sim Tp$ is also a theorem.

R2. If s and $s \to s'$ are theorems, then s' is a theorem too. The Rule of Detachment or of *modus ponens*.

R3. If s is a theorem, then Ts is a theorem too. For example: $Tp \lor \sim Tp$ is a theorem. Hence $T(Tp \lor \sim Tp)$ is also a theorem. The Rule of Truth.

V

We need for our purposes three meta-theorems of our Logic of Truth.

M1. If $s \leftrightarrow s'$ is a theorem of TL, then s and s' are intersubstitutable *salva veritate* in *T*-formulas. This I shall call the Rule of Extensionality or "Leibniz's Law" for truth-logic.

Sketch of a proof. Let $s \leftrightarrow s'$ be a theorem of TL. From the corresponding tautology of PL we obtain the theorem of TL $(s \leftrightarrow s') \to \sim (s \& \sim s') \& \sim (\sim s \& s')$. By the Rule of Detachment we get $\sim (s \& \sim s')$

& ~ (~ s & s'), by the Rule of Truth $T(\sim (s \& \sim s') \& \sim (\sim s \& s'))$, and from this by A3 $T \sim (s \& \sim s') \& T \sim (\sim s \& s')$. From a corresponding tautology of PL we obtain $T \sim (s \& \sim s') \& T \sim (\sim s \& s') \rightarrow T \sim (s \& \sim s')$ whereupon we can detach $T \sim (s \& \sim s')$. To this last we apply A4 and A2 and get $T \sim s \vee Ts'$. By A1 we have $T \sim s \rightarrow \sim Ts$. From the last two formulas, in combination with PL-tautologies and R2, we obtain $\sim Ts \vee Ts'$ and from this $Ts \rightarrow Ts'$. By symmetrical reasoning, applied to $T \sim (\sim s \& s')$ we get $Ts' \rightarrow Ts$. The two implication formulas, finally, yield $Ts \leftrightarrow Ts'$. We have then established that, if $s \leftrightarrow s'$ is a theorem of TL, then $Ts \leftrightarrow Ts'$ is also a theorem of TL. This constitutes the essentials of a proof that provably equivalent formulas of TL are intersubstitutable *salva veritate*.

M2.   Every T-formula is equivalent with a T-formula of the first order, i.e. with one in which no symbol T occurs within the scope of another T.

We sketch a proof of this for strings of symbols T with or without a negation-sign occurring between them. By R1, substituting $\sim Tp$ for p in A5, we obtain $T \sim T \sim Tp \leftrightarrow \sim T \sim Tp$. By virtue of M1 and A5, we can in this formula replace the parts $T \sim Tp$ by $\sim Tp$. This gives us $T \sim \sim Tp \leftrightarrow \sim \sim Tp$. By virtue of A2, we simplify the left member of the equivalence to TTp and by virtue of PL, we simplify $\sim \sim Tp$ to Tp. Herewith we have proved the following theorem:

T1. $TTp \leftrightarrow Tp$.

The theorem says that the phrase "it is true that it is true that" equals "it is true that".[2]

It is now possible, by successive applications of M1, A5, A2, and T1 to contract any string of Ts with or without negation-sign between them to one single occurrence of the symbol T with or without negation-sign in front. The extension of this result to overlaps generally of Ts, whether in strings of immediate succession or not, follows easily from the next meta-theorem.

---

[2] If we had accepted T1 as one of the axioms of TL, A5 would have been provable. This is seen as follows: As already noted (p. 28), $T(Tp \vee \sim Tp)$ is a theorem and provable independently of A5. Hence, by A4 and the definition of disjunction "$p \vee q$" = df "$\sim (\sim p \& \sim q)$" and A2, we have $TTp \vee T \sim Tp$. By virtue of T1 and principles of PL, we obtain from this $\sim Tp \rightarrow T \sim Tp$. The converse is proved starting from A1 and substituting in it $\sim Tp$ for p. We get $T \sim Tp \rightarrow \sim T \sim \sim Tp$. Cancelling double negation by virtue of A2 gives us $T \sim Tp \rightarrow \sim TTp$, and from this and T1 and principles of PL we obtain $T \sim Tp \rightarrow \sim Tp$. Herewith the equivalence $T \sim Tp \leftrightarrow \sim Tp$ or A5 has been proved from T1 and the other axioms of TL. I am indebted to Mr Antti Hautamäki for these observations.

M3. Every *T*-formula is provably equivalent with a molecular compound of atomic *T*-formulas of the simple form consisting of the letter *T* followed either by a single variable or by the negation of a single variable. These atomic formulas will also be called *truth-constituents or T-constituents* of the original *T*-formula.

Sketch of a proof. Consider first an atomic *T*-formula *T*(...). If the expression in front of which the first *T* stands contains signs for disjunction, implication, or equivalence, we replace the parts containing these signs with parts containing only signs for negation and conjunction according to the given definitions. Any occurrence of the letter *T* in the expression thus transformed which stands in front of a conjunction or a negation of a conjunction can now be distributed by virtue of (M1 and) the axioms A3 and A4. Strings of negations may be reduced by virtue of A2, strings of successive *T*s may be reduced by virtue of T1, and occurrences of *T* ~ *T* may be reduced to ~ *T* by virtue of A5. By repeated application of these distributive and reductive operations we reach, in a finite number of steps, a stage when no further distribution or reduction is possible. In the formula with which we have then ended after the transformation all symbols *T* occur immediately before a variable with or without a negation sign in front.

Trivially, by applying the same procedures to all the atomic *T*-formulas of which a given *T*-formula is a compound, we transform the given *T*-formula into a compound of *T*-formulas of the simple kind we have called truth-constituents.

VI

Consider an arbitrary *T*-formula. In it occur in all *n* variables *p*, *q*, etc. The $2n$ atomic *T*-sentences *Tp*, *T* ~ *p*, *Tq*, *T* ~ *q*, etc. are the truth constituents or *T*-constituents of this *T*-sentence. According to M3, the given *T*-sentence is equivalent, in TL, with a molecular compound of its *T*-constituents. (Not all *T*-constituents need actually appear in the compound; missing constituents can, if needed, be vacuously introduced through operations of PL.)

Consider the two *T*-sentences *Tp* and *T* ~ *p*. According to A1, they cannot both be true. If the one is, the other is not. But nothing which we have laid down about TL excludes the possibility that neither of them is true.

The sentences *Tp* and *T* ~ *p* can thus say or not say the true in 3 different combinations. The same holds for the pair *Tq* and *T* ~ *q*. The four sentences can thus say or not say the true in 3 × 3 or 3^2 different combinations. The $2n$ T-constituents of a given T-sentence can be true or not in 3^n combinations.

Since the given T-sentence is equivalent with a molecular compound of its T-constituents, one can use a truth-table to investigate which truth-function of the constituents the sentence itself expresses. If it expresses their tautology, we shall call the given sentence (or the proposition which it expresses) a *truth-tautology* or T-tautology.

Whether the given T-sentence is, or is not, a T-tautology can thus always, after the appropriate transformation of the sentence into a compound of T-constituents, be investigated and decided in a truth-table.

The notion of a T-tautology provides the obvious criterion of *logical truth* in TL.

M4.   All theorems of TL are T-tautologies, and all T-tautologies are theorems of TL.

The proof of this metatheorem is an adaptation of well-known analogous results in modal logic.

VII

Instead of conceiving of the formulas of the T-calculus as two-valued truth-functions of pairs of truth-constituents of the forms Tp and $T \sim p$, Tq and $T \sim q$, etc. we can also interpret them as three-valued "truth"-functions of the variables p, q, etc. themselves. This connects our truth-logic with a polyvalent, in this particular case three-valued logic. Its three values are "true", "false" and "neither true nor false". We can designate them by 1, 0, and $\frac{1}{2}$ respectively. The distributions of the three values over the variables in a table would then be subject to no restriction. The values of the pairs of T-constituents are calculated in accordance with the table below. The calculation of values of compounds of T-constituents then proceeds in the "classical", i.e. two-valued, way.

p	Tp	$T \sim p$
1	1	0
$\frac{1}{2}$	0	0
0	0	1

As shown by the table, the value of a truth-constituent is always either "true" or "false", although the proposition itself, of which the constituent affirms truth or falsehood, may be void of truth-value, be neither true nor false (cf. above p. 25 and p. 28).

VIII

We can now deal with the question of the putative vacuousness of the phrase "it is true that" and of the possible equivalence or non-equivalence of the two Laws of Excluded Middle and of Bivalence respectively.

$T(Tp \leftrightarrow p)$ which would say that the equivalence ("identity") of Tp and p is a truth, is not a theorem of TL. This is easy to grasp intuitively and the reasons we have already given (see above p. 5 and pp. 12f.). But let us look at the matter in more detail by transforming the formula into a compound of T-constituents·

Replacing the equivalence sign by its definition, we first obtain $T(\sim((Tp)\ \&\ \sim p)\ \&\ \sim ((\ \sim\ Tp)\ \&\ p))$.

By virtue of A3, we distribute the T in front of the whole expression and get $T \sim((Tp)\ \&\ \sim p)\ \&\ T \sim((\sim\ Tp)\ \&\ p)$.

By virtue of A4, we distribute the negations in front of conjunctions and get $(T \sim Tp \lor T \sim \sim p)\ \&\ (T \sim \sim Tp \lor T \sim p)$.

By virtue of A2, A5, and TL, we can simplify the last expression to $(\sim Tp \lor Tp)\ \&\ (Tp \lor T \sim p)$ which is the same as $Tp \lor T \sim p$ *simpliciter*.

Herewith has been shown that the two formulas $T(Tp \leftrightarrow p)$ and $Tp \lor T \sim p$ are equivalent. Thus the first would be a theorem of TL if, and only if, the second were a theorem. But the second *is not* a theorem, because, as a truth-table would show, $Tp \lor T \sim p$ is *false* when the proposition that p is itself one which is neither true nor false, i.e. lacks truth-value.

But now it is also clear under which cirumstances the equivalence between "it is true that p" and "p" holds good, i.e. $T(Tp \leftrightarrow p)$ would be a theorem. It holds good if, and only if, it is either true or false that p. So, for propositions which can safely be assumed to have (or are already presupposed to have) a truth-value, the addition of the phrase "it is true that" to the sentence expressing the propositions *is* otiose or vacuous. But it should also once again be clear why an attempt to solve Aristotle's puzzle about future contingencies by a resort to this equivalence "begs the question" (cf. above p. 12f.).

We thus have a theorem of TL which says

T2. $(Tp \oplus T \sim p) \rightarrow T(Tp \leftrightarrow p)$. "If it is either true or false that p, then it is true that it is true that p if, and only if, p."

Another theorem is

T3. $T(p \lor \sim p) \leftrightarrow Tp \lor T \sim p$. "It is true that p or not p if, and only if, it is either true or is false that p."

The proof involves simple applications of A4 and A2. This theorem is the syntactic equivalent of our statement (above p. 11) that the Law of Excluded Middle and the Law of Bivalence actually are but two different expressions of the same logical principle. But it should also be noted that neither $T(p \vee \sim p)$ nor $Tp \vee T \sim p$ are, by themselves, theorems, i.e. logical truths of truth-logic. They are not valid for all propositions, i.e. for all admissible values of the variable "p", whatsoever. They hold good only on the prior assumption that the proposition in question has a truth-value. This condition reduces the statement of the Law of Bivalence to a sheer triviality of PL, *viz.* to $Tp \vee T \sim p \rightarrow Tp \vee T \sim p$. The statement of the conditional validity of the Law of Excluded Middle, *viz.* $Tp \vee T \sim p \rightarrow T(p \vee \sim p)$, can be proved only in TL.

IX

No proposition to the effect that a tautology of "classical" Propositional Logic is true is a theorem of Truth Logic. No tautology of PL, one could say with an air of paradox, is tautologically *true*.

Any substitution instance, however, in TL of a tautology in PL is a tautology of TL. As already noted in passing (above p. 28), we have a theorem

T4. $Tp \vee \sim Tp$.

It says that an arbitrary proposition is either true or is not true. By the Law of Excluded Middle we previously (p. 2) understood the assertion that the disjunction of a proposition and its negation (necessarily) is true—and by the Law of Bivalence the assertion that any proposition (necessarily) is either true or false. We have shown that these two "laws" amount to the same (in TL). We could, if wanted, introduce a slightly revised terminology and decide to understand by the Law of Excluded Middle the principle which says that any given proposition is either true or is not true. This would distinguish the Law of Excluded Middle from the Law of Bivalence and make it possible for us to say that the first is unrestrictedly valid for all propositions whatsoever, whereas the second is not.

As also already (p. 28) noted, since $Tp \vee \sim Tp$ is a theorem, then by the Rule of Truth $T(Tp \vee \sim Tp)$ is a theorem, too. From it is easily derived

T5. $TTp \vee T \sim Tp$.

This theorem says that any proposition of the form of what we have called a truth-constituent is either true or false. Generally: any proposition to the effect that it is true that something or other (is the case) is either true or false. With this too we are already familiar (above p. 28).

A1 is, by PL and A2, equivalent with $\sim (Tp \& T \sim p)$. This again is, by

A3, equivalent with $\sim T(p \& \sim p)$. It is thus a logical truth of truth logic that a contradiction in the sense of PL is *not* true. But it is *not* a logical truth of TL that a contradiction is *false*. $T \sim (p \& \sim p)$ is not a theorem. The formula is equivalent with $Tp \vee T \sim p$ which, as we know, is not a theorem.

Substituting in A1 "$\sim p$" for "p" and applying A2 we obtain $Tp \rightarrow \sim T \sim p$ from which, by A5, we obtain $Tp \rightarrow T \sim T \sim p$. "Truth entails the falsehood of falsehood". But the converse does not hold. Falsehood of falsehood does not necessarily amount to truth.

Some of the above observations will remind one of certain peculiarities of intuitionist logic. (Some further similarities will become manifest when we proceed to quantification.) It seems to me that some of the "intuitions" to which Brouwer gave expression in his philosophy of mathematics are captured and given a natural interpretation in our Logic of Truth and its extension to a Logic of Predication (see below, pp. 42ff.).

X

Someone may find it baffling, or "suspect", that TL should use freely the "inferential machinery" of PL and recognize any substitution instance in TL of a PL-tautology as a T-tautology—and yet refuse to admit as tautologically true any statement to the effect that a PL-tautology is true. But this need not baffle us at all. It is the "point" about TL that it is designed to do justice to the idea that beside declarative sentences which express true or false propositions there are also such which neither say the true nor the false. Accepting this, we must of course also think that molecular compounds of sentences void of truth-value are themselves void of truth-value—even if they happen to have the *form* of tautologies. A compound of the form of a tautology is tautologically true, however, if its atomic constituents are themselves true or false.

p	$\sim p$
T	F
F	T

It is this very assumption, *viz.* that the constituent propositions have truth-value, that underlies the traditional interpretation or modelling of the expressions of PL in truth-tables. Consider, for example, the truth-table above, for negation. How do we argue to this correlation of Ts and Fs? As follows: if it is true that p, we think, then it is false that not-p and if it is false that p then it is true that not-p. And these relations do indeed hold—and can be expressed in the form of theorems of TL. ($Tp \rightarrow T \sim\ \sim p$ and $T \sim p \rightarrow T \sim p$ are T-tautologies.) But what justifies us in thinking that T and F exhaust all possibilities of assigning a value to a given proposition? We just *assume* that propositions take one, and one only, of these two values—not both at once, or neither of them. But this assumption can itself be questioned.

What if instead of "true" and "false" we had said "true" and "not true"? Necessarily, a proposition is either true or is not true, even though it need not be true or *false*. At least this is so according to our truth-logic. ($Tp \vee \sim Tp$ is a T-tautology but $Tp \vee T \sim p$ is not, we have said repeatedly.) We therefore rewrite the truth-table as shown below. Now we can be sure that the two possibilities are at least exhaustive. We then argue: if it is true that p, then it is not true that not-p; and if it is not true that p, then it is true that not-p. But here the difficulty is with the second implication. $Tp \rightarrow \sim T \sim p$ is a tautology of TL, but $\sim Tp \rightarrow T \sim p$ is not. The second implication holds only if it is assumed, not only that the proposition under investigation is either true or not-true, which is trivial, but also that it is either true or false, which is not trivial.

p	$\sim p$
T	$\sim$ T
$\sim$ T	T

So also when the truth-table is constructed in this way, the presupposition is that propositions are true or *false*.

The notion of a tautology, it should be remembered, is a notion of logical *semantics*, not of syntax. A tautology is a propositional compound of a well-defined type which is true for all distributions of truth-values over its components. But in distributing truth-values in truth-tables it is *assumed* or *presupposed* that these components are either true or false and that, if they are true, they are not false, and if false, not true. For this reason one can say that the Laws of Bivalence and of Contradiction are *basic* to the semantics of "classical" PL.[3]

With TL the situation is different. Its semantics does not presuppose the Law of Bivalence. Not any proposition will be either true or false. But any proposition to the effect that a proposition is true will be this, i.e. will

---

[3] On this, the reader is also referred to my early papers "On the Idea of Logical Truth I" (1948) and "Form and Content in Logic" (1949), reprinted in *Logical Studies*, Routledge & Kegan Paul, London, 1957.

be true or false. This is the reason why the T-constituents of any formula of TL can be handled in truth-tables of the "classical" structure. $Tp \vee \sim Tp$ is a theorem of TL and $Tp \leftrightarrow TTp$ and $\sim Tp \leftrightarrow T \sim Tp$ are theorems. Moreover, $TTp \vee T \sim Tp$ is a theorem (T5). It says that it is either true or false that it is true that p.

T5 might be called the Law of Bivalence for truth-constituents.

As for the Law of Contradiction, T-logic does not establish that contradictions, unrestrictedly, are *false* (cf. above, p. 34). They are false only when the propositions contradicting each other are themselves either true or false. $Tp \vee T \sim p \leftrightarrow T \sim (p \& \sim p)$ is a theorem. But a contradiction which is not false is not true either. If a contradiction is not false, then the contradicting propositions are themselves neither true nor false.

But T-logic *does* establish that no proposition is both true and false and also that no proposition is both true and not true. $T \sim (Tp \& T \sim p)$ and $T \sim (Tp \& \sim Tp)$ are T-tautologies, theorems of truth-logic.

Is it necessarily, undeniably, the case that no proposition can be both true and false? Is it inconceivable that a contradiction were, not only not false, but *true*? Is "true contradiction" a "*contradictio in adjecto*"?

The answer is that a truth-logic which is construed as ours does not allow true contradictions. This logic, moreover, appears rather well adjusted to our intuitive notions about truth. But, as I shall next try to show, there are also other—not necessarily "rival"—intuitions which allow us to make sense of the, seemingly, logical monster of a true contradiction.

TRUTH-LOGIC AND "DIALECTICAL SYNTHESIS"

From Dialectical Logic an operation is known which goes under the name of Dialectical Synthesis leading to what is known as the Unity of Opposites (*coincidentia oppositorum*). It can be described as follows:

Let there be a proposition θ. We call it "thesis". Its negation not-θ is then called "antithesis". By some means or other, we disprove the thesis. The thesis is thus not true, $\sim T\theta$. By some means or other, we also refute the antithesis. Thus it too is not true, $\sim T \sim \theta$. From these findings, *viz.* that the thesis is *neither* true *nor* false (= the antithesis true) we now "conclude" that the thesis is *both* true *and* false. This move is called Dialectical Synthesis.

Is the arrow in Zeno's famous *aporia* moving or at rest at a given moment of time? Arguments may be produced to show that it is not moving—but also to show that it is not at rest. Therefore: the arrow is both moving and at rest.

Can we "make sense" of this? Before answering the question, we turn attention to the following:

Consider the proposition that it is raining. In order to have a truth-value the proposition must be "individuated" in space and time. How? In a big area or over a long period of time it may be both raining and not raining— although not "at the same place" and "at the same time". "It was raining in France in 1980" would normally mean that it was raining at at least one place in France at at least one time in 1980. The proposition that it is raining in (all) Paris the (whole) afternoon on 5 November 1980 may be true or false. Assume that it *is* true. Now consider a very small spot in a street of that city. It was during that afternoon hit by only one or two drops of water or perhaps not by a single drop. Even two drops of water would not be "rainfall". So did it after all not rain in all parts of Paris that after-noon? What counts as a "part" of a city? Hardly a few square inches in a street. Or consider a very short interval of time. Perhaps not a single drop fell in any part of Paris during that time on that afternoon. So was it, after all, not raining the *whole* afternoon? The very notion of rainfall, one would wish to say here, is a "macroscopic" notion which has an applica-tion only to regions in space and time of a "fair size". To very small regions the notion is inapplicable. For some values of s and t it is neither true nor false to say that it is raining in s at t.

Incidentally, does not the Heisenberg uncertainty relation mean that the notions of position and velocity cease to be applicable in spatio-temporal regions of extremely small size? Would it not be better to express oneself thus than to say, as is sometimes done, that the idea of spatio-temporal location itself becomes inapplicable?

The idea of becoming (*das Werden*) has an important place in the philo-sophy of Hegel. It is the case that p at t and that $\sim p$ at the later time t'. In between these two times that p changed to that $\sim p$. When did the change take place? Sometimes the question can be answered with great exactitude, i.e. with a preciseness which meets all practical needs (to know when a certain thing happened). But if the process is of a "macroscopic" kind, then there will be an interval of time within the interval $t-t'$ when it is not possible to tell whether it was *still* the case that p or *already* the case that $\sim p$.

Related to the notion of becoming are those of beginning and stopping and of continuous and gradual change.

A huge number of processes are such that they lead from a state of affairs which is univocally such that p to one which is univocally such that $\sim p$ through a "zone of transition" in which it is neither true that p nor that $\sim p$. I assume that societal change is often, perhaps usually, of this kind.

Rainfall, too, exemplifies such a process. It has been raining for some time in a certain area. Then it stops. But, let us assume, not all of a sudden, but "gradually" so that there is a "period of transition" when one could not say that it is raining nor that it is not-raining. However, when viewing things from the point of view of there being absolutely no drop of rain falling in the region, we might include the "period of transition" in the period of rainfall and say that it was still raining until the weather was absolutely dry. But similarly we could say that it was raining only as long as it was "clearly" raining and when it became "uncertain" it was in fact no longer raining. It is as a matter of linguistic usage not at all uncommon or unnatural to say that in such a "period of transition" it is both raining and not raining. Such locutions are often used. They are sometimes used to create an impression of puzzlement, as when in the fairy tale the princess appeared in a fishnet—neither dressed nor undressed and thus both dressed and undressed.

One can, when speaking about such things as rainfall, distinguish between a *strict* use of the phrase "it is true that" and a *laxer* use which covers also the borderline cases, if there are any. And similarly for the phrase "it is false that (true that not)". For the strict notion of truth we have the symbol T. For the relaxed notion I shall use the symbol T'.

The two notions are interdefinable. To be true in the laxer sense simply means not to be false in the strict sense—and to be true in the strict sense means not to be false in the more liberal sense of "true" and "false". Thus we have

$$T' p =_{df} \sim T \sim p$$

and

$$Tp =_{df} \sim T' \sim p.$$

As we know, for the notion of strict truth the Law of Contradiction holds good: no proposition is both strictly true and strictly false. But the Law of Excluded Middle does not hold: a proposition may be neither strictly true nor strictly false.

For the relaxed notion of truth the situation is the opposite. The Law of Excluded Middle holds for this notion, meaning that every proposition is either in the laxer sense true or in the laxer sense false, i.e. $T' p \vee T' \sim p$ for any value of "p". But the Law of Contradiction does not hold universally: some propositions are, in the relaxed sense, both true and false, i.e. $T' p \& T' \sim p$ for some values of "p".

Since the two notions are interdefinable, any T'-formula can become translated into a T-formula and tested for truth (tautologicity) in truth-logic. The truth which is at stake in this test is the *strict* notion of truth. Thus, for example, it is *strictly* true that every proposition is, in the *relaxed* sense, either true or false.

If there is no "zone of transition" separating that p from that $\sim p$, the two notions of truth coincide. Their coincidence means that the Laws of Contradiction and Excluded Middle (Bivalence) are both valid and we are "back" in Classical Two-Valued Logic of Propositions.

Thus underlying the operation of thought called Dialectical Synthesis is *a shift in the* (use of the) *concept of truth*. Without this shift the operation makes no sense. No proposition can be neither true nor false and, at the same time, both true and false *in the same sense* of "true and false". But they can be the first in one sense of "true" ("false") and the second in another sense, both senses making "good sense".

The idea of Dialectical Synthesis seems in the first place applicable to contexts involving the concepts of becoming, of change, and of process. But the idea of the two notions of truth, a "strict" and a "laxer" one, has also application in contexts of *vagueness*.

A great many concepts used in discourse about contingent matters of experience are not sharply bounded but have a "fringe of vagueness" (corresponding to a "zone of transition" in the case of changes and processes) which accounts for the existence of "borderline cases" of which it is hard to tell whether they fall under the concept or not. "Hard to tell" does not here point to limitations of our epistemic faculties of ascertaining and observing things. The phrase refers to the absence of *criteria* for applying the concepts to the case at hand.

Sometimes attributes (colours for instance) "shade into one another" and it is tempting to say that something falling in the fringe of vagueness of two such concepts (say red and orange) falls under neither and yet also under both. The object then falls *strictly* under neither concept and *in a laxer sense* under both.

It is possible that such observations as the above scratch only the surface of the depths of Dialectical Logic. But the fact that our attributions of truth can "oscillate" in a way which answers to the move of thought called Dialectical Synthesis seems to me interesting and also worth a more detailed formal-logical study than given to it here.

Truth-Logic and Antinomies

It is easily shown that the following is a theorem of TL: $T(p \leftrightarrow q) \leftrightarrow Tp \,\&\, Tq \vee T \sim p \,\&\, T \sim q$. If it is true that two propositions are (materially) equivalent, then and then only they are either both true or both false. Since falsehood entails not-truth (A1) we also have the theorem $T(p \leftrightarrow q) \rightarrow Tp \,\&\, Tq \vee \sim Tp \,\&\, \sim Tq$. If two propositions are equivalent, then they are either both true or neither of them is true.

Can a proposition be equivalent with the assertion of its own falsehood? Then one would have $T(p \leftrightarrow T \sim p)$.

By the first of the above theorems $T(p \leftrightarrow T \sim p)$ is equivalent with Tp & $TT \sim p \vee T \sim p$ & $T \sim T \sim p$. This reduces to Tp & $T \sim p \vee T \sim p$ & $\sim T \sim p$. Both disjuncts, as we know, are refutable in TL. Thus we have proved $\sim T(p \leftrightarrow T \sim p)$. The answer to our question above is No. It cannot be true that a proposition is materially equivalent with another which says that the first proposition is false.

By the second of the above theorems $T(p \leftrightarrow T \sim p)$ entails Tp & $TT \sim p \vee \sim Tp$ & $\sim TT \sim p$ which is equivalent in TL with Tp & $T \sim p \vee \sim Tp$ & $\sim T \sim p$. But the first disjunct is refutable in TL. Hence $T(p \leftrightarrow T \sim p)$ entails $\sim Tp$ & $\sim T \sim p$. A proposition which was equivalent with the assertion of its own falsehood would be neither true nor false. (Such a proposition would *not* be both true *and* false—except in the "weak" sense of truth and falsehood which also covers propositions without truth-value. However, the idea of a "dialectical synthesis" does not seem applicable, or of interest, in this case.)

By contraposition, we can maintain $Tp \vee T \sim p \rightarrow \sim T(p \leftrightarrow T \sim p)$. This says that a proposition with a truth-value cannot be equivalent with the assertion of its own negation.

A proposition can of course *say* of itself that it is false. "This proposition is false" = "p". Which proposition? This same proposition, that p. So that, if Tp then also $TT \sim p$, i.e. $T \sim p$. Thus $Tp \rightarrow \sim Tp$ which entails $\sim Tp$. But also, if $TT \sim p$ then Tp or $T \sim p \rightarrow Tp$ which entails $\sim T \sim p$. The proposition which says of itself that it is false thus necessarily (provably) is neither true nor false.

One could define an *antinomic proposition* as follows:

A proposition is antinomic if, and only if, from the assumption that this proposition is either true or false it follows logically that, if it is true it is false, and if it is false it is true.

Thus, if the proposition that p is antinomic we have, in truth-logic, $Tp \vee T \sim p \rightarrow (Tp \rightarrow T \sim p)$ & $(T \sim p \rightarrow Tp)$. This can also be written in the form $Tp \vee T \sim p \rightarrow \sim Tp$ & $\sim T \sim p \vee T \sim p$ & $\sim T \sim p \vee \sim Tp$ & $Tp \vee T \sim p$ & Tp. The second and third disjunct in the consequent are refutable in PL and the fourth in TL. Hence the consequent reduces to $\sim Tp$ & $\sim T \sim p$. But this is the negation of the antecedent $Tp \vee T \sim p$. A (material) implication the consequent of which is the negation of the antecedent is logically equivalent with the consequent alone. This allows us to infer the consequent from the implication. The inference was called by the medievals the *consequentia mirabilis*.

Thus we can infer, by the *consequentia mirabilis*, that if a proposition is antinomic then it lacks truth-value, is neither true nor false.

The idea that antinomic propositions lack truth-value is, as such, no novelty. It may be said to be the "point" of various constructions and devices such as Type Theory or the Vicious Circle Principle or restrictions on definitions and concept formation to remove antinomic propositions from the realm of truth and falsehood. But what is interesting, and perhaps novel, is that this removal can be effected without these restrictive constructions by the instrument of Truth Logic alone.

The Logic of Predication

I

In the *Prior Analytics* (51b23−24) Aristotle observed that "'to be not-good' and 'not to be good' are not the same". In other words, he is making a distinction between denying that something has a certain attribute or property and affirming that it has what may be termed the negation of that property.

This distinction is related to the one which we have been making here between denying that a proposition is true and affirming that it is false. The affirmation entails the denial. For, as Aristotle goes on to say (52a1−2), "if it is true to say 'it is not-white', it is also true to say 'it is not white'". But not vice-versa, since then not to be white would be the same as to be not-white. "The negation of 'it is true to call it white'", Aristotle acutely observes (52a33−35), "is not 'it is true to call it not-white' but 'it is not true to call it white'".

It follows from the distinctions which Aristotle is making that not everything has either a given property or has the negation of this property. Something may neither have the property nor its negation. As Aristotle says at the very end of the chapter concerned (52b32−33): "The negation of the good is the not-good; and the not-good is not identical with the neither good nor not-good."

It would be rash to maintain that Aristotle's distinctions coincide with the ones we are making here. They are interestingly similar but hardly identical. I have, for example, not found in Aristotle any clear indication that he wished to identify the falsehood of a proposition with the truth of its negation and thereby distinguish between the denial of truth and the affirmation of falsehood of a proposition.

II

Something which is not-white can also be said to *lack* the property of whiteness. To be white and to be not-white are thus cases of having a property and lacking it, respectively.

A thing which, as the case may be, either has or lacks a given property will be said to be in the *range* of the property concerned. Logs and pieces of cloth are in the range of the property whiteness—and so are all things and stuffs which are or may be coloured.

The range of a property can also be spoken of as its *range of significance*. If a certain thing neither has nor lacks a given property, then the attribution of this property to this thing "makes no sense" or "is meaningless".

The number 7, to be sure, is not brave. This, however, does not mean that it lacks braveness, is something of a coward. It means that numbers just do not belong in the range of significance of attributions of traits of character to something.

Sometimes the lack of a property has a special name in language, making the distinction between having and lacking arbitrary. Thus, for example, the number 7 may be said to "lack" the property of being an even number—on the ground that the proposition that 7 is an even number is *false* (not "meaningless"). By virtue of this we can say that 7 *has* the property of being not-even. This property, however, has a name of its own, "odd".

III

Hitherto we have used letters *p, q,* etc. to represent entire declarative sentences. For declarative sentences of the subject–predicate form we shall now use complex symbols, consisting of a capital letter *A, B,* etc. followed by a lower-case letter *a, b,* etc. The capital letter stands for an adjective, for example "red", "square", or "brave", or for a noun phrase of the type "a man", "a prime number", etc. The lower-case letter stands for the name or the phrase used for referring to that thing of which is predicated the property signified by the adjective or noun phrase represented by the capital letter. For example, "7", "the author of Waverly", or "Napoleon".

Aa is read "*a* is *A*", *TAa* is read "it is true that *a* is *A*", ~ *TAa* says "it is not true that *a* is *A*", and *T* ~ *Aa*, finally, "it is true that *a* is not *A*" or, which is the same, "it is false that *a* is *A*". It should be observed that, since we are using the letter *T* to mark the distinction between denying that something has a property and affirming that it lacks it, we do not need the hyphen to distinguish between, say, "it is not white" and "it is not-white".

When we are dealing with a molecular compound of schematic subject–predicate sentences all of which have the subject in common, we may contract the schema into a compound of capital letters within brackets followed by a single occurrence of the lower case letter. For example: we may write (*A* & *B*)*a* as shorthand for *Aa* & *Ba*. This device has an equivalent in ordinary language. Instead of saying "he is brave and he is wise" we may say "he is brave and wise", treating "brave and wise" as a compound adjective.

IV

We now proceed to *quantification*.

From books on logic we are familiar with symbols like $(Ex)Ax$ or, $\lor Ax$. It says that there is something which is A. E or $\lor$ is called the existential quantifier.

Quantification is a sophisticated logical device, the meaning and nature of which is not at all easy to clarify. In order to understand matters here, it is important to keep clear the connection with ordinary language.

Sticking to our previous conventions, Ax should be read: "x is A". In conformity with this, one could suggest the following reading of the symbol $\lor Ax$: "there is (exists) an x such that x is A". Whether this is a grammatically correct sentence may, I think, be questioned. The troublemaker here is the phrase "an x". What does it "mean"?

One way of making the reading grammatically flawless would be to say "there is something such that it is A"—and then substitute for "A" an adjective, e.g., "red". Another, handier, reading would be "there is something which is A" or simply "something is A". But for the sake of logical perspicuity I shall stick to the clumsier reading of the quantifier "there is something such that".

Now consider the pronoun "it" in the sentence. It refers back to the thing which, so to speak, is hiding anonymously under the indefinite label "something". Therefore we cannot replace it by the name of some definite thing. We are being told only that there is a thing such that when its name is put in the place of "it" and the quantifier phrase "there is something such that" is dropped then the resulting sentence expresses a true proposition.

The sentence "it is red", for example, is like the sentence "it is raining" in that it requires a supplementation before it yields a true or false proposition. With this supplementation the sentence is *closed*, without it it is *open* (see above, p. 24).

The supplementation needed for closing an open sentence is often provided by the context. "It is raining" without further specification of when and where would normally be understood to mean that it is raining now and here—and the "it" in "it is red" would normally refer to an individual spoken of or pointed to in the context.

There are two principal linguistic devices, it seems, by which an open sentence may be closed. The first is through the naming or describing of some (logical) individuals. In the case of "it is red", the "it" is then replaced by a name or a definite description. In the case of "it is raining" the sentence is supplemented by a reference to a location in space and time. The second device for closing a sentence is the operation called quantification. In the case of "it is red", quantification means prefixing either the phrase "something is such that" or "everything is such that" or "nothing is such that" to the sentence. In the case of "it is raining" it means adding to the sentence one of the nine possible combinations of words

somewhere		sometime
everywhere	and	always
nowhere		never.

The open or closed character of a sentence is not changed by adding to it the phrase "it is true that". "It is true that it is red" is as much of an open or a closed sentence as "it is red". But "there is something such that it is true that it is red" is a closed sentence. We could introduce the symbol E or $\vee$ for the phrase "there is something such that". If "A" stands for the adjective "red", the above sentence could be expressed in symbols "$\vee T$ it is red" or shorter "$\vee T$ red it" in conformity with our convention to read "Aa" as "a is A". Finally, we can replace "it" by the symbol for a variable "x" and get "$\vee TAx$". This is how I shall proceed, in agreement with familiar practice. But actually, the use of the variable instead of the pronoun is not necessary for our purposes as long as we are dealing only with open sentences of the subject–predicate form and their quantification. When we deal with sentences of the relational form such as, for example, "a is a friend of b" we need a device for differentiating between the "its" under the "something".

V

The range of significance of the property A is constituted by all things which either have or lack this property, i.e. by the totality of things which are such that when their names are put in the place of the variable we obtain a truth-expressing sentence from the schema $TAx \vee T \sim Ax$. The range of significance may be empty. This is expressed by the formula $\sim \vee(TAx \vee T \sim Ax)$. If a thing is not in the range of A then its name satisfies the open sentence $\sim (TAx \vee T \sim Ax)$ or its equivalent form $\sim TAx \, \& \sim T \sim Ax$. If the range is empty, then there is no thing the name of which satisfies the sentence $TAx \vee T \sim Ax$ or, which shall by definition be regarded as saying the same, all things are such that their names satisfy $\sim (TAx \vee T \sim Ax)$.

Instead of $\sim \vee \sim (TAx \vee T \sim Ax)$ we shall also write $\wedge (Tax \vee T \sim Ax)$. $\vee$ is the existential, $\wedge$ the universal quantifier.

Assume that the range of A is not empty, i.e. that it is true that $\vee (TAx \vee T \sim Ax)$, but that no thing in the range nor, needless to say, outside it *lacks* the property in question. Then we have $\sim \vee T \sim Ax$. This in combination with the fact that there are things in the range of A, amounts to saying that every thing in the range of A is A. Since the range is not empty, what is said can also be expressed by the formula $\vee TAx \& \sim \vee T \sim Ax$. Shifting from the existential to the universal quantifier we can write this as follows: $\sim \wedge \sim TAx \& \wedge \sim T \sim Ax$. In words: it is *not* true of every thing that it does not have the property A but it *is* true of every thing that it does not lack the property A.

When we say that every thing has a certain property what we ordinarily mean is, I think, that every thing *in its range* has it—and not that every thing which *there is* has it. We can introduce a special symbol for this "restricted" universal quantifier, let us say U. Thus $U TAx$ is an abbreviation for $\vee TAx \& \sim \vee T \sim Ax$.

There is thus a certain asymmetry between existence and universality. This was often implicitly felt but perhaps never quite clearly brought to light.

The truth of $\vee TAx$ warrants that there are things in the range of A and that some thing in this range actually is A. $\wedge TAx$ has a much more sweeping content. It says, *not only* that every thing *in the range of A is A, but also* that every thing *there is* is A. Now if some thing is A then this thing is in the range of A. So that if it were true that $\wedge TAx$, the range of A would comprise the totality of all things. Normally this is not the case with properties. Therefore we seldom say such things as "every thing is . . ." but indicate the range by some qualifying attribute. We say, for example, "all material bodies are heavy", thereby indicating that weight is a property restricted to matter and that all material bodies possess it. But every thing is not matter.

If the range of a property is empty then, on the traditional view of handling quantification, one would have to say that every thing in the range has the property in question and also that every thing in the range lacks it. Both A and $\sim A$ are "universal" in the range. But nobody whose speech is not corrupted by the jargon of logicians would say this.

Existence and universality form an exclusive and exhaustive pair in the sense that either some thing has a given property or every thing is such that it has not got it. In symbols: $\vee TAx \vee \wedge \sim TAx$. Thus if it is not the case that every thing is such that it has not got a given property, then some thing has this property. These relations seem to me clear and uncontroversial.

The situation is different when universality is restricted to the range of a property. From the proposition that every thing is such that it has not got a given property it does not follow that every thing lacks this property. $\vee TAx \vee \wedge T \sim Ax$ is not a truth of logic. Hence one cannot, from having established, one way or another, that it is not the case that all things lack a given property, conclude that there is some thing which has it.

One can see this also from considerations relating to the idea of restricted universality. To deny that every thing in the range of the property A has this property, $\sim UTAx$, is tantamount to affirming the disjunction $\sim \vee TAx \vee \vee T \sim Ax$, i.e. tantamount to affirming that either there exists some thing which lacks the property in question or there does *not* exist any thing which has it. In order to pass from the refutation of the universal proposition that $UTAx$ to the affirmation of the existential statement that $\vee T \sim Ax$ we must also refute the statement that $\sim \vee TAx$, i.e. we must establish that there exists some thing which has the property the "restricted" universality of which is being denied. Thus in order to pass from the refutation of the statement of universality to the affirmation of the statement of existence we must first establish the truth of another existential statement.

These findings are related, I think, to doubts raised by intuitionists concerning the use of inverse proof for establishing statements of mathematical existence. In order to establish that *some* number has (lacks) a certain property it is not enough to have established that *not all* numbers lack (have) this property. The refutation of the universal statement must concern numbers *in the range* of the property under consideration, i.e. numbers to which, as one would also say, it "makes sense" to attribute the presence or the absence of this property. That there are numbers in this range must be known or established independently before we can draw existential conclusions from the refuted statement of universality.

VI

That the range of a property is empty means that no thing has and no thing lacks this property: $\sim \vee TAx \, \& \sim \vee T \sim Ax$. Shifting to universal quantifiers we have: $\wedge \sim TAx \, \& \wedge \sim T \sim Ax$. Then it is also true of any given individual thing, say a, that $\sim TAa \, \& \sim T \sim Aa$, i.e. the proposition that a is A is neither true nor false.

Are there properties the ranges of which are empty?

Self-contradictory properties would hardly qualify as examples. Consider for example the "property" of being a square circle. No thing has this property. But any thing of which it is true that it lacks the property of squareness or lacks the property of circularity would fall in the range of the property of square circularity. A triangle might be an example of such a thing. If we accept that a triangle is a not-square or a not-circle we may conclude that the range of the property of being a square circle is not empty.

48 *The Logic of Predication*

Some attributes might be called "fictional", for example to be a centaur or a chimaera. There are no centaurs—but are there things (animals) which are "not-centaurs", which lack the property of centaurhood? (Perhaps a lion could be said to be a not-tiger.) Could one not examine some animals and find that they are *not* centaurs? The idea seems sensible only if animals were known to exist which could be mistaken for centaurs. Then the range of this particular property would not be empty.

Let it be that we coin an adjective "prom" and said "*a* is prom". No criteria for judging whether a thing is prom or not are provided. Shall we say then that promness exemplifies a property with an empty range? If one takes the view that "*a* is prom" is a well-formed subject–predicate sentence, then it would be in order to say that the proposition that *a* is prom lacks truth-value and that promness exemplifies a property with an empty range. If, on the other hand, one excludes "*a* is prom" from the class of well-formed English sentences, one cannot speak of the proposition which it expresses or of the property of promness. It seems to me that both ways are open to us. One can "recognize" "prom" as an adjective and "*a* is prom" as a subject–predicate sentence—or one can refuse to do this. Our calculus caters for the possibility that one does the first. But one must not let oneself be mystified by the "existence" of nonsense properties like, e.g., promness.

Also with centaurs it seems that there are two possibilities. One can take a "realist" attitude to centaurs and say, for example, that all animals (or all mammals) are not-centaurs. Or one can take a "fictionalist" attitude and say that no animal, nor anything else, is a centaur or is a not-centaur.

VII

That the range of a property is universal means that every thing either has or lacks this property. In symbols $\wedge(TAx \vee T \sim Ax)$. By the rules of truth-logic this can be written $\wedge T (Ax \vee \sim Ax)$ and by our convention above about molecular names of properties this can be written $\wedge T (A \vee \sim A)x$.

Are there properties the ranges of which are universal?

$TAa \vee T \sim Aa$ must not be confused with $TAa \vee \sim TAa$. The first is true if, and only if, the thing *a* has or lacks the property A. The condition is satisfied provided that *a* falls in the range of A. But the range of this particular property need not be universal. Thus it may happen that $TAa \vee T \sim Aa$ is void of truth-value, is neither true nor false. But $TAa \vee \sim TAa$ is a (truth-)logical truth whether *a* falls in the range of A or not.

$TAx \vee \sim TAx$ is thus true, one would say, for all "values" of the variable. One could use a quantifier for indicating this. A traditional way of writing this would be $(x) (TAx \lor \sim TAx)$. The reason why I do not wish to use, without further motivation, the symbol $\lor$ for the quantifier is that this type of quantification is not covered by our introduction above (pp. 44f.) of quantifiers attached to subject–predicate sentences. $(A \lor \sim A)x$ is a schematic subject – predicate sentence, and thus also its expanded form $Ax \lor \sim Ax$, but $TAx \lor \sim TAx$ is not.

Thus the universal validity of the schema $TAx \lor \sim TAx$ cannot be taken as showing that there are properties the ranges of which are universal. If it could be thus taken, the range of *every* property would be universal.

The question which we are raising is related to problems about "logical types". In the normal cases, the range of significance of a property is restricted to things of a certain "type", e.g. lengths to distances, shapes to surfaces and solid material bodies, colours to visible objects or stuffs, etc. A number is not 1 yard or more or less than 1 yard long, my headache yesterday was neither white nor not-white. Sometimes it may be difficult to tell whether things of a certain type should be counted as belonging to the range of a given property or not. But in the normal cases, it is possible, for any given property, to give examples of things which fall in its range and also of things which are outside its range. Thus, in the normal cases, the ranges of properties are neither empty nor universal. But whether this is necessarily so and for all properties without exception is a question which I shall not attempt to settle here.

VIII

A name may be without bearer, a descriptive phrase not denote any existing thing. Examples: "Pegasus", "the King of France", "the greatest cardinal number". Also such names and phrases often figure as the subject-terms in subject–predicate sentences.

Of some such sentences it seems natural to say that the propositions which they express are neither true nor false. The proposition that the greatest cardinal number is an even number is not true. But nor is it false—which would mean that the greatest cardinal number is an odd number.

What about the propositions that Pegasus is a horse or that Pegasus is a mythological animal (horse)? *In some sense* they are true. One is tempted to say, moreover, that the second is even "more true" than the first. But what about the proposition that Pegasus is an ambler—or that Hamlet had an elder brother? It is being understood that "Pegasus" refers to the said mythological animal and "Hamlet" to the prince in Shakespeare's play. Is there any evidence for or against either statement? I assume not.

But may not ancient manuscripts be discovered which would show that Pegasus was commonly held to be an ambler and could there not have existed another version of the play, in which Shakespeare had endowed Hamlet with an elder brother? The answer presumably is Yes—but what weight would such evidence carry for the question of truth of the propositions under consideration?

I strongly doubt whether questions such as these have a univocal answer. Several attitudes to them seem possible. One could give an account of fictional names, or of names without bearer generally, which would lead one to deny that such statements as that Pegasus is a horse are either true or false—but also an account which leads one to pronounce all such statements false, and one which pronounces them true or false "as the case may be". And for this reason alone, I should say, it is important to build a Logic of Truth which caters for the possibility that some propositions may *truly* (or falsely) be said to lack truth-value.

IX

In the traditional predicate calculus there is a rule known as the rule of existential generalization. It can be paraphrased as saying that if it is true that a is A then (it is also true that) something is A. In our symbolism this would be written $TAa \rightarrow \vee TAx$. Accepting this in our calculus we should, by virtue of the Rule of Truth (above, p. 28) also have $T(TAx \rightarrow \vee TAx)$ from which one can deduce $TAa \rightarrow T \vee TAx$.

In the traditional calculus which does not distinguish between lacking a property and not having it, the rule also permits the inference from that a is not A to that some thing is not A. From having the formula above in our calculus one can, by substitution, derive $T \sim Aa \rightarrow \vee T \sim Aa$ which says that if a lacks the property of Aness then some thing lacks this property. But one could not derive the formula $\sim TAa \rightarrow \vee \sim TAx$ which says that if it is *not* true that a is A then *there is* some thing to which it is not true to attribute the property in question.

The formula $\sim TAa$, as we know, covers two cases. One is when the proposition that a is A is false. The other is when the proposition is void of truth-value. In the first case the existential inference is warranted. In the second it is not.

The mere fact that the proposition that a is A lacks truth-value does not show that there is not a thing such that this proposition is not true. If the thing named "a" is not in the *range* of the property then there is (exists) some thing which is not in this range. But if "a" does not name any thing and, *on this ground*, the proposition that a is A is pronounced void of truth-value, then the existential inference would be false.

The case when the subject-term of a subject–predicate sentence does not name any ("existing") thing is notoriously troublesome. On the Russellian analysis, "the King of France is bald" turns out to express a *false* proposition—but not one the form of which is "$T \sim Ax$". This analysis could be extended to concern, not only definite descriptions, but proper names as well. "Pegasus is a horse" would then express a false proposition—and also "Pegasus is a not-horse".

In another way of understanding the sentences the appropriate thing to say is that the propositions which they express lack truth-value.

In neither of these cases, however, would an existential generalization of the kind which the rule $TAa \rightarrow \vee TAx$ allows be warranted.

If we accepted the inference from $\sim TAa$ to $\vee \sim TAx$, then we could by contraposition, and after shifting from the existential to the universal quantifier, derive $\wedge TAx \rightarrow TAa$. But this formula is not valid in the quantified Logic of Predication which we are here studying. This fact may be said to constitute a noteworthy difference between this logic and the traditional predicate calculus.

Determinism and Knowledge of the Future

I

As we have seen, the Law of Excluded Middle—and its equivalent the Law of Bivalence—has presented a problem relating to determinism. It has been thought that the unrestricted validity of these laws would force us to accept that the truth of everything that is or will be is predetermined. I have tried to show that this "deterministic illusion" originates from a misconception of the idea of truth—and that the mist is dispersed when this idea is made clear.

There is an analogous problem or puzzle connected with the idea of *knowledge*. It has been thought that the existence of an omniscient being—such as the Christian God is conceived to be—is incompatible with the notion of man as a free agent. More particularly, it has been thought that foreknowledge or knowledge of what is going to be entails the predetermined truth of its object. I hope to be able to show that *this* "deterministic illusion" has its root in a misconception of the notion of knowledge.

II

One can distinguish *personal* and *impersonal* knowledge. The first is in question when we say that *N.N. knows* (or that I know) that so and so (is the case); and second when we say that *it is known* that so and so.

(There are also many more distinctions to be made when speaking about knowledge, for example between knowledge *that*, knowledge *whether*, knowledge *which*, knowledge *how*, and knowledge *of* (something). Some of these distinctions too will concern us later.)

Personal and impersonal knowledge are logically related to one another. If something is known, then somebody knows it. But somebody may know something without this thing being known. Impersonal knowledge is, somehow, "public". This does not mean, however, that what is impersonally known is known to everybody. It may, on the contrary, be known only to very few, say a small group of experts or scientists.

Assume that everything which is true were also known. Then, by the above, every truth is such that at least somebody knows it; but from this it does not follow that there is somebody who knows everything. Suppose, however, that there existed such an omniscient being, a "God". It would not follow that then there is impersonal knowledge of every truth; because God's knowledge need not be, presumably could not possibly be, what we call "public" knowledge. Perhaps it has to be in some essential way "private".

It is questionable whether the notion of omniscience (an omniscient being) involves a logical contradiction. But I do not think that the question of its consistency need trouble us here. Our problem is not whether omniscience is logically possible but whether knowledge of what will be entails or presupposes that the future is predetermined. In the discussion of this question the idea of an omniscient being may be entertained as a useful fiction.

III

A claim to know something is normally based on some grounds ("grounds for knowing"). The grounds, roughly, are what constitute a truthful reply to the question *how* something is known.

Grounds of knowledge are sometimes something which we have *experienced* or *ascertained*. I know that N.N. is in town today. How? The answer might be that I saw him in the street a short while ago (an "experience") or that I telephoned him to make sure that he was at home (a result of ascertaining a fact).

Grounds of knowledge are often something we accept on *trust* (in somebody). How do I know that N.N. is in town? Somebody told me so. How do I know that Napoleon died in St Helena? I was taught so at school and I have read it in history books. How do I know that there will be an eclipse of the moon next Monday?—an example among many of something we claim to know about the future. Answer: This is what is said in my astronomical almanack for the year. No doubt the majority of things we know, we know "on trust".

A ground for knowledge, one could say, is something which we *unquestioningly* take for granted at the time when we claim to know something. That which we unquestioningly take for granted I shall call a *certainty*. Grounds of knowledge are thus what I call certainties.

Grounds may be questioned. Imagine the following dialogue: "Are you sure it was *him* you saw in the street and not somebody very like him?" "Yes, absolutely. We stopped and talked for a while." "But might he not have left town since you met him?" "It is barely one hour since I saw him; as a matter of fact he said he was going to have lunch in a nearby restaurant." "But can't he have changed his mind?" "I have no reason to think so; have you?"

Or imagine this conversation: "You say you were taught at school that

Napoleon died at St Helena. Was everything you were taught at school true then?" "Perhaps not everything, but I certainly have no reason to doubt this particular item. Beside I have read it in books on history. The fact is common knowledge; nobody doubts it."

In both the imagined conversations there is not only mention of grounds in support of my claim but reference is also made to the *absence* of grounds, as known to me, for not trusting my grounds or for doubting the thing I claim to know. This "negative moment" associated with claims to knowledge is, I think, both characteristic and important.

Sometimes, however, questioning the grounds given in support of knowledge will prompt us to reconsider the situation. Was it perhaps somebody else who answered when I telephoned to make sure that he was at home? Maybe there is a misprint in my astronomical almanack? When such doubts arise and are taken seriously we suspend our previous claim to knowledge until we have settled whether the doubts are justified. When such settlement takes place there is again something which we un-questioningly take for granted and which now is the *ground* for our acquired *knowledge* that the thing we first referred to as a ground for a claim to knowledge either is true or not. If true, the claim stands; if false, the claim will be dropped or remain in suspense.

I am absolutely sure that Napoleon died at St Helena. It is common knowledge shared by historians. No-one outside the circle of people who conduct investigations into the history of mankind could "possibly" doubt this. That is: we should regard someone who questioned this fact as "crazy". But suppose some day a historian came up with what seemed conclusive evidence that Napoleon in fact did not die at St Helena but that the British, shortly before the death of the ex-emperor, moved him to Isle of Man and that he died there. Can we not imagine this—is it not "possi-ble"? I think we must admit that no barrier of a logical nature blocks out imagination here. But if the imagined possibility were to come to be an ac-cepted item of common knowledge of history, it would have to stand on a greatly revised basis of certainties which no serious historian would then question. (Documents relating to the transfer of the ex-emperor, etc.)

IV

Is it (logically) *possible to know* the future, what is going to be?

Before trying to answer the question we must make more precise the no-tion of "what is going to be".

Propositions of logic and mathematics are, somehow, "removed" from space and time. Knowledge of them (their truth) is not knowledge of what is going to be. I know that there will be a sea battle tomorrow or will not be a sea battle tomorrow—but this is not genuine "knowledge of the future".

The laws of nature again are not "removed" from space and time, they are rather *semper et ubique*, i.e. always and everywhere. Shall we say that knowledge of them is or involves knowledge of what is going to be? In order to answer this question one would have to scrutinize in detail the logical form of natural laws and also whether such laws can be genuine objects of knowledge at all. Many philosophers would deny that such knowledge is possible and some would support their view with a reference to the anticipatory character of laws of nature. I shall later try to argue that knowledge of natural laws is *not* knowledge of what is going to be.[1]

Objects of genuine knowledge of the future must be *contingent facts*. Exactly what this means is not, however, easy to say;[2] but a criterion of contingency which is at least a *sufficient* one can be formulated as follows:

A state of affairs or an event is contingent if it is of a generic character such that states (events) of this character sometimes obtain (happen), sometimes not. For example, that it is raining in a certain place or that a certain person is sitting is in this sense contingent. If it were known today that it will be raining in Paris tomorrow this would be (genuine) foreknowledge.

Such contingencies, however, may at the same time be necessities of a sort. Many things which happen, happen by virtue of what is often called "causal necessity". This presumably means that there are "laws of nature" such that, under the then prevailing circumstances, it was, given those laws, (logically) necessary that the thing in question was going to be (obtain, happen, take place).[3] Rainfall, whenever it occurs, may be of this character. Such things I shall call *contingent necessities*. The case when a man is sitting is perhaps different. We do not feel much inclined to say that whenever a man is sitting, he is sitting "of causal necessity". A believer in determinism, however, would maintain that *all* such contingencies are contingent necessities. He could, of course, not dispute that it sometimes is raining and sometimes not and that, this being so, the *generic* proposition that it is raining is contingent. But since whether it is raining or not in a certain place at a certain time is a matter of necessity under natural law, any *individual* proposition to the effect that it is raining is not contingent but, if true, necessary and, if false, impossible.

---

[1] In the essay "Laws of Nature", below, pp. 134ff.
[2] For a more detailed discussion of this, see below, pp. 96, 100 and 115.
[3] See below, p. 136.

V

It seems that knowledge of (some) future contingencies is possible. To deny this would be to deny that something is "knowledge" which commonly passes under that term.

Let us here survey some examples of what could reasonably count as knowledge of what is going to be:

(a) It is night now, but I know that in a couple of hours it will be daybreak.

(b) Astronomers know that there will be an eclipse of the moon at *t*. It can be predicted with great exactitude. (A classical example.)

(c) I knew that the text which I was jotting down on a sheet of paper when writing this was going to remain legible for a considerable time; that it would not fade away as soon as I had finished writing.

(d) I know that if I jump out of the window of a tall building I shall fall to the ground and hurt myself badly, perhaps be killed. I know that if I put my hand in the fire, it will hurt.

(e) I know that I shall die some day in a not very distant future.

The epistemological status of all these examples deserves careful consideration.

VI

In (a) and (b), our knowledge that a certain event will occur is, it seems, grounded in our confidence that certain processes in nature—the rotation of the earth round its axis, the revolution of the moon round the earth and the earth round the sun—will continue undisturbed. We are certain that these processes go on stably, and on the basis of this we (say we) know that such and such events will occur at such and such times.

When describing the grounds on which our expectation of daybreak is based it is not, however, necessary to refer to any explanatory hypothesis concerning, e.g., the rotation of the heavenly bodies. It is sufficient that there is familiarity with ongoing processes in nature, and no reason for us to assume that they will change or stop. There need not be any particular reason, however, why we think that they will go on (for ever). We simply are confident that the processes will continue as in the past—at least "for the time being".

In both examples, *viz.* the one that there will be daybreak soon and the one that there will be an eclipse of the moon at a certain time, we are confident that some things will *not* change and on this ground we say we *know* that certain other things *will* change (night to day, etc.). Something speaks against calling our conviction that the earth will continue to rotate, the sun not soon get extinguished, etc., *knowledge*. The more appropriate name seems to be to call it a *certainty*. It is something which unquestioningly we take for granted, without asking for grounds. But astronomers can (perhaps) be said to *know* that after so many billions of years the sun will be extinct and for such knowledge grounds are requested.

VII

The case (c) is of a similar nature as the cases (a) and (b) but reflects something even more basic about the fabric of human knowledge. We are confident that certain things will *not* change but continue to *be*. Our whole life is based on confidence of this character. The concept of human action, the idea that men can act, is based upon it. When I attribute to myself the action, say, of opening a door, I am, normally, prepared to say that, had it not been for my interference, the door would not have opened. The door which I can truly be said to have opened *myself*, did not open *of itself*, i.e. under the influence of some cause for its opening of which I was unaware. Sometimes the implicit certainty or confidence I felt can turn out to have been deceptive—but mostly this does not happen. If it happened frequently with me in regard to a particular kind of action, it would affect my claim to be able to perform this action. And if it happened frequently with most people in regard to most actions, it would upset our whole view of action and agency. These concepts would totter.

My confidence in this particular instance (c) of a "uniformity of nature" is also connected with my acquaintance with the stuff called "paper" and the instruments called "pen" and "pencil" and with the activity we call "writing" (of which "jotting down" is a form). I *know how* to write (*can* write, have been taught to write) and I *know which* utensils are required for practising the art.

Only under special circumstances would one use the locution "know that" in such cases. Ordinarily we take things here for granted, treat them as certainties, do not question our confidence in them. In order even to conceive of them as of things we *know*, somebody or something must *challenge* or shake our confidence. If somebody for no particular reason challenged my confidence that the script which I am jotting down will stay on for some time, I should probably not understand him. I should perhaps think that he is not familiar with the activity of writing and the utensils used in practising it. Or think that he is a philosophical sceptic and that I ought to meet his challenge by philosophical arguments. A *reason* for challenging my confidence might be, for example,[4] that I had for some time been using alternatingly two different kinds of ink: one normal, and one which quickly vanished or turned illegible (perhaps because I wanted it thus). If my interlocutor were unsure which ink I am *now* using he might challenge my claim, had I made one, that the script will stay on and not vanish. If I then say, with emphasis, that I *know that* it will not vanish, my reason for saying thus might be that I am sure which ink I was using.

When a regularity or uniformity of the kind exemplified by (c) did not hold good in the past we were usually able to *explain* why it failed to hold—for example, whenever a script did not stay on but vanished we could attribute the vanishing to a "cause" and need not have to think that it happened "of itself". But when, in the individual case, we are confident that the regularity in question will hold good this is because we have then *no reason* to expect an exception to the rule, and not because we *have reasons* to expect the uniformity to continue in the case at hand.

VIII

Case (d) as we stated it, is not primarily a case of knowledge of the future, but of acquaintance with a uniformity on the basis of which future things may be anticipated with certainty. "Fire hurts." This, ultimately, is inductively acquired knowledge—although some of us may never have experienced it themselves but only learnt it from others. Someone grabs my hand and forces it into the flame. I *know* that this is going to hurt. This, if anything is "knowledge of the future". But what of the hypothetical—i.e. that *if* my hand is put into the fire I shall be hurt? Is my knowledge of it not knowledge that a certain "disjunctive state of affairs" will continue to obtain, *viz.* that either my hand stays away from the flame *or* I shall be hurt? How can I know this? Are there not exceptions? Surely there are. The burning stuff can be of a kind which burns at a too low temperature to be hurtful. Or the nerves in my skin may have been prepared in a way which makes them insensitive. All this is possible. But only seldom, if ever, have such contingencies arisen in *my* experience. When, in a concrete situation, I am absolutely confident that if I then put my hand in the fire it is going to hurt, this means that I have *no* reason for thinking that this situation is exceptional, not of the normal kind. This can be called knowledge of a disjunctive state prevailing for the future, i.e. for the future I am now facing—not perhaps for "all future" and any conceivable situation.

---

[4] I owe this example to Professor Norman Malcolm.

IX

Consider finally case (e). Surely we know *that* we shall die. But we usually do not know exactly *when*. I am *sure*, in any case, this will be before A.D. 2010. But do I (GHvW) *know* this too? I should, considering my present age and what I know about my state of health, hesitate to say that I *know* this. What of my dying before 2050? One hears about people, who, reputedly, lived to be 150 or thereabout. But I should not hesitate to say that I know I am not one of those Methuselahs. *How* do I know this? What can I say in reply? I have no special grounds for my knowledge. So perhaps I cannot, after all, be *quite sure* that I shall not live to be 134 myself?

Reflecting on such questions as those above throws light on knowledge of the type exemplified by man's mortal nature. It is inductive knowledge of a sort. Its experiential basis is our acquaintance with some common natural processes of a limited duration, such as the life-spans of men and animals, the passing character of gales and rainfalls, the regular intervals between sowing and harvesting, etc. It would be unsound philosophic eccentricity to deny that this is a sufficient basis for (some) *knowledge* of what is going to be.

Such knowledge, however, is not "causal". There is no point in qualifying my knowledge that I shall die by a clause saying "unless certain processes go on for ever". We are certain they won't. But it makes sense to say that I know that men *normally* die before they are 100, or that the seeds sown in the spring will *normally* mature for harvest by autumn. If a man lives to be 70 we do not (normally) ask what made him live to that age—but if he lives to be 100 or more we may be curious. We look perhaps for some "causal factors" which can be held "responsible" for this—such as that he kept a certain diet or had an exceptionally strong heart. And if the seeds which were sown never resulted in mature crop there must, we are sure, have been a cause why this did *not* happen. And we know many such possible causes—for example an abnormally early frost.

X

Must knowledge be based on grounds? More particularly: if someone knows what is going to be, must he have grounds for his knowledge?

Assume there existed a soothsayer or "oracle" whom we consult about the future—about matters generally or about matters of a certain sort, such as the weather. Will it be thus and thus tomorrow, say raining? Let us assume that he always, or nearly always, replies and that he *always*, without exception is right. We should speak of this person as someone who knows about the future (weather). But suppose he has no grounds. We ask him—and the answer just comes. He can say nothing about *how* it is that he knows. Nor can we. Are we then not misdescribing the case if we still seriously maintain that he knows? Ought we not to say that he is extremely good at divining or *guessing* things—but not that he knows? On the other hand, why not say this if he is an absolutely reliable source of information about the future? Would we not then, on some occasions, say that *we know* that there will be rainfall tomorrow and, when asked, *how we* know this, answer that we consulted the oracle? This indeed is how we would express ourselves—and this seems unobjectionable. The oracle's answer is *our* ground of knowledge. So why not then say of *him* that he knows?

It is no objection to retort that there *are* no such oracles—and that if there were they would be, for example, skilled meteorologists who have extremely solid grounds for their weather forecasts. This may be true—but nothing seems to stand in the way of thinking that things *were* as in our imagined case of the soothsayer. So the question still is: Would *he* know?

A possible move here would be to say that things known without grounds—whether about the future or about something else—are not properly *known* either. They are just taken for granted, held to be certain. They are the *certainties* which provide grounds for anything which can properly be said to be *known* (cf. above pp. 53f.).

Many of the things which Moore in his famous essay claimed to know are "certainties" in this sense. For example that I have two hands (as known to me). Not all such Moorean certainties, however, are provided by "the evidence of our senses". For example, my knowledge of my own name or that the earth existed long before I was born is of a different kind.

One can thus drive a wedge between knowledge and certainty such that it becomes true by definition that all knowledge is based on grounds. And then one would say of our oracle that what is going to be tomorrow is to him a *certainty* and of us that we *know* what is going to be because we trust in the oracle. Expressing oneself in this way does not sound unnatural. But I should myself prefer a more liberal mode of expression and count the certainties as cases of groundless knowledge.

Our attitude to the imagined case of the "oracle" we could perhaps best describe as follows:

We do not know on what grounds, if any, he knows. But we trust him; like a child may trust his parents or an elder brother or sister. He is our authority. We rely on him completely and it does not occur to us to question his grounds or to ask whether he has any. We may even think it improper to do so. It may also be considered impudent to ask him too many questions; but we are confident that he has answers to them all.

An omniscient God would be like an authority in such a position. That is to say: our idea of an omniscient God is, I think, modelled in analogy with a human knower and with human knowledge, i.e. knowledge ordinarily based on grounds. The idea of groundless knowledge of the future is an analogical extension from cases of grounded knowledge.

XI

Assume that it is known at t' or that somebody knows at t'—the distinction between the impersonal and the personal case now being immaterial—that it will be the case at t that p. For this I shall introduce the symbol $K_{t'}p_t$ & $t' < t$. For sake of brevity, I shall henceforth omit the term $t' < t$ in the conjunction.

We have the internal relation (entailment) $K_{t'}p_t \rightarrow p_t$. It holds irrespective of how t' and t are related—and therefore also when it is the case that $t' < t$.

It makes no sense to say that one knows that something is the case but that perhaps it is not the case after all. (But if for "knows" we put "believes" the sentence makes sense.)

The person who says that he knows this or that is making a *claim*. A claim can be justified or not. How does one decide, come to know, whether a claim to knowledge is justified?

If, contrary to the claim, it turns out not to be, say, the case at t that p, the person cannot have *known* at t' that p at t. But he might nevertheless have been *justified* on the basis of the grounds he had to make the claim that he knew this.

Someone tells me: "I know that he will come tomorrow. He promised and he is extremely reliable." Having heard this we make all kinds of arrangements and preparations for his visit. But he does not turn up. We wonder whether the speaker really was justified in claiming to know that he would come. We reconsider the case. Perhaps we come to think that he was *not* justified. He ought perhaps to have taken into account that the expected visitor's mother had died in the meantime and that thereby he had an overriding reason for not fulfilling his promise to us. But perhaps we come to think that he *was* justified in making the claim, even though the object of knowledge did not materialize. He *could not reasonably have foreseen*, we say, that which made the expected visitor break or leave unfulfilled his promise.

Someone says "I know he will come tomorrow". But we feel doubtful. The grounds on which the claim to knowledge is made seem to us unconvincing. Perhaps the putative knower can support his claim, if at all, only by saying something like "My intuition tells me that he will come". And the expected visitor comes. The question whether the claim to knowledge was justified may remain open to debate. Perhaps we must think that although the person was right, meaning that that which he asserted will happen actually happened, his claim was nevertheless not justified on the grounds he had. But did the person who made it *know*? Someone may wish to say that he did not know, he only made a good guess. (As one might say about our "oracle" above that it does not know the future but only invariably guesses correctly.) But perhaps the guesser himself does not share this opinion, "I *knew* he would come; I told you so." Must we deny that he knew if he cannot support his claim with acceptable reasons? Must we say he knew, only if he can justify his claims by pointing to such reasons? The answer to neither question seems to me obvious. If, for example, on many similar occasions he had claimed to know something but been mistaken, then an exceptional case when he is right would hardly be one in which we should say that he "knew".[5] If he is notorious for always being "cocksure" of things regardless of whether they turn out to be true or not we might be inclined to dismiss his claim and say that he only *pretended to know*. But if, for whatever reason, he is a person who "enjoys our confidence" then, if he claims to know that something is going to happen and this thing happens then we might say that he *knew* that it was going to happen even though he would not have been able to justify his claim to knowledge by giving any reasons at all or reasons which justify the claim. But then he must also stand by his claim—and not weaken it by saying such things as, for example, "I think", "I have a hunch", "I predict" or something similar which would be compatible with saying "But I do not *know*".

XII

I have argued for the importance of upholding a distinction between claiming to know, justifying a claim to knowledge and knowing.

To justify a claim to knowledge is to state the grounds on which the claim is based. These grounds may be questioned and it may be found out or thought that they did not justify the claim. But from this it does not follow that the person who made the claim did not *know*.

But if this is so why bother about justifying claims to knowledge at all? The answer is that most claims to knowledge are based on grounds which

---

[5] I am indebted to Professor Norman Malcolm for this observation.

are, rightly or wrongly, thought to justify them. The grounds are what normally makes us feel sure or confident in our claim. By giving the grounds we try to convince others that things are as we claim to know they are. And it may be important for us, and for others, that we have the same beliefs about certain things.

But to the question whether we knew what we claimed to know it is not essential whether we had grounds or not for the claim or whether the grounds we gave justified the claim or not. Essential are two things. The first is that things are as we claim we know they are. The second is that the claim is serious or *sincere*. The seriousness of a claim to knowledge is tested not only by what we say, "profess", to know. It is also a commitment to take such actions and precautions which we agree are called for or reasonable. There may be grounds for questioning the seriousness of a claim and the result of a test of seriousness may be open to different interpretations. But often there is no reason to doubt the seriousness of a claim to knowledge. If then the thing turns out true, the person who made the claim *knew* what was going to be—whether he could give reasons or not.

XIII

If it is contingent whether p at t then the truth of $K_t \cdot p_t$ *depends* on whether p at t. What does "depend" mean here? It means, I suggest, that if somebody at t' *claims to know* that p at future t then his claim cannot be *settled* (decided) until t.

A claim to know what is going to be at t may be disputed—and the one who disputes it can persist disputing it until the time is there. The claim is settled on the basis of ascertaining facts at t. This is itself an epistemic process. It may but need not lead to a settlement of the disputed claim. If it does not, the person who disputed the claim may persist disputing it. The claim may also be settled later, on the basis of ascertaining the past.

I shall not here inquire into the nature of the epistemic processes through which claims to knowledge are settled. Let it only be said that they are verificational procedures for coming to know something on grounds which are (logically) *independent* of those grounds, if there were any, on which the settled claim to knowledge was itself based.

That somebody's *claim to know* at t' that p at future t cannot be settled until t does not mean that one could not *know* at t', that one knows that p at t. That $K_t \cdot K_t \cdot p_t$ can be *true* just as that $K_t \cdot p_t$ can be true. But the former too depends on whether p at t—if p at t is contingent. One can know what is going to be and know that one knows this—but a claim to have such knowledge can only be settled at t, or—possibly—later.

Does $K_t \cdot p_t$ entail $K_t \cdot K_t \cdot p_t$? Generally speaking: if I know something, do

I then also know that I know this thing? This is a bewildering and much debated question. I shall not discuss it here in full. This much seems certain, however: if someone *claims* to know something then he thereby also claims to know that he knows this thing. "I know that he will come." "Are you not only making a conjecture?" "No, I know." This last "I know" is tantamount to a claim that I know that I know. "I know that he will come but I do not know that I know this" is either nonsense or logically false. If we treat it as a logical falsehood, we should have to treat "it is not the case that I know that he will come but do not know that I know this" as a logical truth. This last is equivalent with "I either do not know that he will come or know that I know this". So therefore, if I know that he will come I also know that I know this. One would then have to say that the first person statement "I know—" *when used for making a claim to knowledge* entails the claim that I know that I know.

One can, however, know things without claiming to know or reflecting on one's knowledge of them. One can also be unsure whether one knows this or that. I used to know most plants which I saw when I went roaming in the woods, i.e. I used to be able to identify them by their Latin names. Do I still know them? I go for a walk and find that I have forgotten many of them. But also that I still know a good many. *Now* I also know that I know them. But *before* I set out on the walk? Surely I knew them then too. But did I know that I knew them? The obvious answer seems to me to be No. Thus I can know something at *t* without knowing, at *t*, that this is the case.

(Knowing or remembering a name is not propositional knowledge. But knowing that *this* plant which *now* I see is a — is such knowledge. And it was in order to test it that I set out on a walk.)

XIV

It should now be clear in what sense foreknowledge *depends* on the future, on what is going to be; and therefore also that the future does not depend on our knowledge of it. This is but a special case of a general thesis that knowledge of a contingent truth is contingent—and in this sense "dependent" upon that truth.

This holds true also of God's knowledge. The idea of an omniscient being who knows everything which contingently is going to be (including all "contingent necessities") may not be a self-contradictory idea. It is questionable, to say the least, whether one can associate the idea of claiming to know with the notion of God. God does not "claim" to be omniscient, nor does he claim to know this or that. If God revealed to a human being that *p* will be at *t*, then that person may claim to know this—on the ground that God revealed it to him. But this claim might be contested and have to be settled when the time is there.

If we believe in an omniscient God and if it so happens that *p* at *t* we can say: since God is omniscient he will have known this ahead of time. This, however, is no ground for saying that things are true *because* God knows them. God knows them because they are true and he is omniscient.

The argument that God's foreknowledge cannot rightly be said to determine the future hinges upon our acknowledgement that there are genuine *contingencies*—counting as contingencies also the "contingent necessities" under natural law. Not to admit the existence of contingencies is tantamount to thinking that everything which is or happens is non-contingently necessary. But this again would be incompatible with the existence of genuine *fore*knowledge (cf. above, p 55).

XV

We shall now apply the above insights to action and free will.

If *x* knows at *t'* that *y* will perform a certain action *A* at *t* then (it is certain that) *y* will do *A* at *t*. If *x* has the knowledge in question, *y* cannot fail to do *A* at the appointed time; cannot omit doing it.

If God knows whether I shall sin or not, no resolve on my part not to sin will make any difference to what I do. If, in particular, what he knows is that I shall sin, *I* cannot prevent my fall.

Thus it may appear that, if the epistemic situation is as described, then it does not *depend* upon the agent himself whether he will do the action or not. Since *y* cannot fail to commit the action, it would be futile for him to try to omit it. His action seems predetermined.

Such thoughts as these may seem—have seemed to people—persuasive. They are, of course, sheer confusion. One need not disprove the existence or doubt the omniscience of God in order to avoid the fatalistic consequences for our action. The task is to show that these consequences do not follow.

One could cut short the discussion by referring to what has already been established about foreknowledge, and say as follows: God knows my future actions, but *what* he knows about them depends upon the character of these actions and not the other way round: the character of the actions upon God's knowledge of them. My actions are not going to be what they are going to be "because" God knows them, but since God knows them they are going to be according to his knowledge.

But saying this will hardly remove anybody's feeling of puzzlement here.

XVI

Why does the fact that *x* knows at *t'* that *y* will do *A* at *t* not "determine" *y*'s action? The question is: on what does it *depend* whether *y* will perform a certain action, or not?

This depends first of all on *y's abilities*, whether he can do this *kind* of action or not. Often he must have learnt (how) to do it and he must normally also know the "meaning" of the action, i.e. when it is appropriate to do it or for what purpose one may undertake to do it. These are features of the agent which exist independently of whether, on the individual occasion in question, the agent proceeds to action or not.

Secondly, the occasion must provide an *opportunity* for the action. Whether it does depends on the concrete situation in which the agent happens to be (and to the creation of which the agent himself may, or may not, have contributed). One cannot open a door which is already open, nor answer a question which has not been asked.

These conditions about ability and opportunity being satisfied, the agent *may* (can) do the action. Whether or not he *will* do it depends upon factors of what might be called a *motivational* nature. The agent perhaps has some reason for doing the action—for example that he thinks it conducive to something he covets or that he is obliged to do it by some moral or legal rule or commitment. Then he may do it *for that reason*. But he may have the same reason and yet not do the action—for example because of some reason or reasons *against* doing it. Or he may have no reason *for* and some *against* doing a certain action, and abstain. He may also do or abstain *for no particular reason*—and this either in the *absence* of reasons for or against or in the presence of such reasons which, however, he chooses to neglect.

"You had promised." "Yes, I ought to have done it." "So why did you not do it?" "I don't know, I just did not do it." A psychologist may conjecture an explanation ("subconscious reason") for the abstention and be right—but the case may also be, as we should say, "inexplicable".

What was just said about the motivational factors and the way action depends upon them is part of our picture of man as (free) agent.

An agent has *no* reason *for* doing a certain thing and *some* reason *against* doing it. He does the thing *in order to* show that he is free to act against his reasons. But then he had a reason for acting as he did, *viz.* that he thereby vindicates his freedom. If he had not had *that* reason he would not have acted as he did. This sort of "uprising against reasons" therefore is no "proof" at all that man is free.

XVII

We can now state our conclusion about foreknowledge and freedom of action. God (or somebody else) may know that the agent *y* is able to perform actions of the kind *A* and that at *t* there will be an opportunity for him to do an action of this kind. God also knows exactly which reasons for and which reasons against doing this action *y* will have at *t*. Moreover, God knows how *y* will react to these reasons, i.e. whether he will do the action or not then. God thus knows everything on which the agent's action can be said to *depend* and also whether the agent will do the action or not. But that does not mean that the agent's action would in any sense *depend* upon God's knowledge of what is and is going to be. What God knows about the future depends upon what will be—*if* what will be is contingent.

Knowledge and Necessity

I

Genuine foreknowledge, we said (above, p. 55), must be of future contingencies. It was also mentioned (p. 64) that if the object of knowledge is contingent, then knowledge of it is contingent too. The proof of this is as follows:

What is known is true. Thus if what is known is that p_t and if this is known at antecedent time t', we have $K_{t'}p_t \rightarrow p_t$. This, moreover, is a necessary truth. Thus we have, using the symbol "N" for "it is necessary that", $N(K_{t'}p_t \rightarrow p_t)$ which according to uncontroversial principles of modal logic entails $NK_{t'}p_t \rightarrow Np_t$. By contraposition, we have $\sim Np_t \rightarrow \sim NK_{t'}p_t$. Shifting from a statement of necessity to one of possibility and using for the latter notion the symbol "M", we can write this $M \sim p_t \rightarrow M \sim K_{t'}p_t$. Since it is contingent that p_t we have $M \sim p_t$ and thus, by *modus ponens*, $M \sim K_{t'}p_t$. But we assumed that $K_{t'}p_t$. Hence, by uncontroversial principles of modal logic, we also have $MK_{t'}p_t$. The conjunction $MK_{t'}p_t$ & $M \sim K_{t'}p_t$ means that it is contingent whether, at t', it is known or not that p at t. This completes our proof.

In view of what has just been proved it may be objected that our previous discussion has missed the point of the medieval problem in philosophical theology. For surely, it may be said, God is not only omniscient but he is this necessarily. Hence, if he knows that p at t, he necessarily knows this. Thus, in his case, $NK_{t'}p_t$. And then we derive from the formula which we already have established Np_t. Thus, the argument goes, God's foreknowledge actually *is* incompatible with the existence of contingencies.

But this argument is fallacious. Let it be agreed that God necessarily knows the future. What this means in terms of foreknowledge, however, is that he, at t' necessarily knows *whether* it will be the case that p at t or not. (And this is so for every value of t, t' and p.) Therefore one of the two things, that p at t or that $\sim p$ at t is necessarily known to him at t'. But this only means that $N(K_{t'}p_t \lor K_{t'} \sim p_t)$ and from this it does *not* follow that one of the disjuncts is necessarily known by God to be true—and therefore it does not follow that it is necessary either.

So it seems that the necessity of God's omniscience is fully compatible with the contingent character of the things themselves which he knows. Then it is contingent too that he knows *that* that which is true is true, although it is necessary that he knows *whether* it is true or not.

I think that this is an acceptable way of reconciling the necessary omniscience of God with the existence of genuine contingencies. In other words: that God's knowledge of contingent facts is contingent is fully compatible with that it is necessary that he knows them. I am not myself sufficiently versed in the theological discussions to know whether this solution of what seems at first a difficulty is acceptable to Christian theology. But it seems to me of interest in as much as it shows that even though God necessarily knows what is going to be, i.e. whether it is going to be this way or not, no deterministic conclusions follow from this, since it does not follow that what is going to be is going to be of necessity.

II

Knowledge of contingent truths must itself be contingent knowledge. But knowledge of necessary truths may, as far as logic is concerned, be either contingent or itself necessary.

Let it be the case that the knowing subject necessarily knows whether a given proposition or its negation is true and that this proposition itself or its negation is necessary, and not contingent. Then the subject also knows that the proposition which is necessary is true. But is his knowledge of its truth necessary? Thus, in particular, if God necessarily knows whether any given proposition is true or not, does he then necessarily know all necessary truths? The question is worth looking into:

The premiss is $N(K_{t'}p_t \vee K_{t'} \sim p_t)$. If it is, say, necessary that p at t, then it is impossible that not p at t, or $Np_t \rightarrow \sim M \sim p_t$. But since a known proposition is true and an impossible proposition false, it follows that an impossible proposition cannot be known (to be true). In symbols: $\sim M \sim p_t \rightarrow \sim K_{t'} \sim p_t$.

Since what is necessary is also true, it follows from our premiss above that $K_{t'}p_t \vee K_{t'} \sim p_t$. This in conjunction with $\sim K_{t'} \sim p_t$ entails $K_{t'}p_t$. Thus we have $N((K_{t'}p_t \vee K_{t'} \sim p_t) \& Np_t \rightarrow K_{t'}p_t)$ which in its turn yields $N((K_{t'}p_t \vee K_{t'} \sim p_t) \& Np_t) \rightarrow NK_{t'}p_t$ which, finally, gives $N(K_{t'}p_t \vee K_{t'} \sim p_t) \& NNp_t \rightarrow NK_{t'}p_t$.

This shows that God necessarily knows the necessarily true only on condition that the necessarily true is *necessarily necessary*, i.e. that if Np_t then also NNp_t.

It used to be one of the disputed things in the philosophy of modal logic whether the necessary entails its own necessity, or not. The answer, in my opinion, depends upon what "type" of necessity is involved. Some necessity is itself necessary; other necessity is contingent. It is, moreover, feasible to think that *logical* necessity is of the former type, but that *natural* or *physical* necessity is of the latter. Accepting this we could say that God, since he necessarily knows whether any given proposition is true or not, also necessarily knows all logically necessary truths but not all "natural", i.e. contingent necessities. Knowledge of them is contingent knowledge.

III

If we entertain the idea of an omniscient being at all, it also seems natural to combine it with the idea that his omniscience pertains to him of necessity rather than by contingent accident.

Man is not omniscient, but he knows various things—including things about the future. Is part of his knowledge necessary, another part contingent? *Can* the notion of necessary knowledge be applied to man at all? The question may be divided in two:

(1) Are there propositions such that a man necessarily knows *whether* they are true or not?
(2) Are there propositions such that a man necessarily knows *that* they are true?

One might think that some objects of what is often called "immediate" knowledge are of the first type. For example, a man may be said necessarily to know whether he has toothache or not—leaving possible borderline cases out of account. When he has toothache he knows this, but it does not follow that he necessarily knows this. (Since then it would be necessary that he has toothache—and this can, at most, be a contingent necessity.) But he may still be thought necessarily to know whether he has or has not toothache at any given moment.

It has been doubted whether immediate knowledge deserves the name "knowledge" at all. It is not knowledge based on grounds. I cannot support a claim to know that I have toothache by anything else but the fact that I have (feel) it. "I have toothache" says the same as "I know that I have toothache". "I know" is vacuous or otiose—in a way reminiscent of "it is true that" in front of a sentence expressing a true or false proposition. My certainty that I have toothache should therefore perhaps not be called knowledge. But once we see how it *differs* from knowledge based on grounds, there seems no harm in using for it that name. Accepting this, I think that man, as far as immediate knowledge is concerned, *is* "like God" in the sense that he may be said necessarily to know whether things stand this way or not—though not to know necessarily that they stand as they do.

This "likeness of man to God" is also a clue, I venture to suggest, to certain philosophical ideas which have, at times, been associated with the idea of God. It has been said that God's omniscience is like an immediate awareness of or *in-sight* into things past, present, and future. So that he has, as it were, only to turn his look at things in order to see whether they stand a certain way or not—just as we, in an act of "introspection", can decide whether we have a headache or not. Such an idea of omniscience may be difficult to understand; perhaps it does not even make sense. A point about God which is more palatable to our understanding is, I think, that his knowledge is direct in the sense that it is not based on grounds. Grounds go, as I have said earlier, with *claims* to knowledge—and it seems inappropriate to attribute such claims to God (cf. above, p. 64). His knowledge, one could therefore say, is *certainty*—and, if one is keen on separating knowledge and certainty—not "knowledge" in the genuine human sense.

IV

As we have seen, if a truth is necessarily known, then it is a necessary truth. So our second question above (p. 70) therefore is whether there are necessary propositions which are necessarily known.

Someone may know a necessary proposition without knowing that it is necessary. I cannot see on what grounds it may be thought plausible, or might even be proved, that any man must know about some propositions that they are necessarily true (contingently or non-contingently). Must the concept of necessary truth be part of any man's "epistemic equipment"? I doubt this. But it is certainly not unplausible to think that any man will know a good many truths which are, in fact, necessary—some contingently necessary, others necessarily necessary. It may, moreover, be (logically) necessary that any man should know *some* such truths. This may be a feature of the notion of a knowing subject. But it is hard to see that there are any specific truths which are such that any man necessarily knows *them*. Therefore I incline to think that the answer to our question (2) above is negative.

"Omne quod est quando est necesse est esse"

I

In the wonderful ninth chapter of *De Interpretatione* we read (19a24−25): Τὸ μὲν οὖν εἶναι τὸ ὂν ὅταν ἦ, καὶ τὸ μὴ ὂν μὴ εἶναι ὅταν μὴ ἦ, ἀνάγκη. Boethius, in his commentary, renders this in Latin as follows: "esse quod est, quando est, et non esse, quando non est, necesse est". In the commentary by St Thomas Aquinas we find this, more elegant, rendering of the first half of the Aristotelian thesis, "Omne quod est necesse est esse quando est". The formulation with the slightly changed word order in the title of the present essay was used by Ockham in his commentary on *De Interpretatione*.

This thesis has been the subject of much commentary and exegesis, also in modern times. What I shall say about it does not claim to be a hypothesis about what Aristotle "meant" by his words. In fact, I think that he did *not* mean exactly what I have in mind here. My aim is to suggest an interpretation which makes the thesis itself appear plausible and to discuss some aspects of the thesis, thus interpreted, which seem to me of interest. For my purposes I am also going to make a free use of other things which Aristotle says in the ninth chapter or elsewhere, and which elucidate his thesis on, as I shall call it, *the necessity of the present*.

II

One should note the qualification *quando est*. Aristotle does not say that everything which is (true) is this necessarily. He says that it is necessary *when it is*. Shortly after the quoted sentence he says (19a26−27) that it is not the same thing to say that what is must be when it is, εἶναι ἐξ ἀνάγκης ὅτε ἔστι and to say that it is, in itself, necessary ἁπλῶς εἶναι ἐξ ἀνάγκης. That which is necessary when it is may very well be contingent in itself.

The statement that at time *t* it is the case that *p* will be symbolized by "p_t". "*p*" is a schematic representation for a sentence which describes a generic state of affairs—for example that a sea battle is being fought or that Socrates is sitting. Let "*N*" denote necessity. The Aristotelian thesis which we are discussing *seems* to say something like $p_t \rightarrow N_t p_t$ or that, if *p* at *t* then it is necessary at *t* that *p* at *t*.

That it is "in itself" or *simpliciter* necessary that *p* at *t* might be symbolized by "Np_t". And that it is necessary that *p* *regardless of time* or, as one could say, *atemporally* necessary that *p*, might be symbolized by

"Np". It is not clear whether the Aristotelian ἁπλῶζ εἶναι ἐξ ἀνάγκηζ, when used of a state of affairs, better answers to the meaning of "Np_t" or of "Np".

One possible way of understanding the idea that a state of affairs necessarily obtains "independently" or "regardless" of time is to mean by it that this state *always* or *omnitemporally* obtains. In symbols: Λp_t. On this interpretation of ἁπλῶζ εἶναι ἐξ ἀνάγκης the statement that a generic state is possible would mean that it *sometimes* obtains (Vp), that a state is impossible that it *never* obtains, and that a state is contingent, finally, that it sometimes obtains and sometimes does not obtain.

Such an interpretation of the modal notions which rests upon an identification of necessity with omnitemporality is nowadays sometimes called "statistical".[1] Hintikka has argued forcefully in several publications that Aristotle understood modality *simpliciter* (ἁπλῶς) statistically. Whether this is right or not, it is obvious that thinking about the modal notions in "statistical" or, better, temporal terms is characteristic of Aristotle and of the medieval Aristotelian tradition in logic.[2]

In addition to the three cases denoted symbolically by "$N_t p_t$", "Np_t" and "Np" there is also a fourth case, "$N_t p$". This last says that it is necessary at time t that the (generic) state that p obtains. This idea of necessity—and corresponding ideas about the other modal notions—can, I think, be adequately related to a view which is well known from the Ancient tradition and associated mainly with the name of the Megarian logician Diodorus Cronus. According to Boethius,[3] Diodoros held that

---

[1] The term was coined by Hintikka in connection with his research on Aristotle's views of modality. See, e.g. his book *Time and Necessity*, The Clarendon Press, Oxford, 1973, p. 103. The same term for the same idea had been used earlier by Oskar Becker in his *Untersuchungen über den Modalkalkül*, Westkulturverlag Anton Hain, Meisenheim am Glan, 1952. The statistical interpretation of modalities must not be confused with the interpretation, familiar from so-called possible worlds semantics, of necessity as truth in *all*, possibility as truth in *some*, and impossibility as truth in *no* possible world. Just as the statistical interpretation may be traced to Aristotle, the possible world interpretation goes back to Leibniz. Becker, surprisingly, confuses the two interpretations. He writes (*op. cit.*, p. 18): "Leibniz hatte bereits in seiner Lehre von den möglichen Welten . . . eine statistische Theorie der Modalitäten gegeben." ("Leibniz, in his doctrine of possible worlds . . . had already given a statistical theory of the modalities.") This is not the case.

[2] This has been shown in detail by Simo Knuuttila in *Aika ja modaliteetti aristotelisessa skolastiikassa* (Time and Modality in Aristotelian Scholasticism), Annales Societatis Missiologicae et Oecumenicae Fennicae, Helsinki, 1975 and *Duns Scotus ja mahdollisuuden "statistisen" tulkinnan kritiikki* (Duns Scotus and the Criticism of the "Statistical" Interpretation of Possibility), Reports from the Institute of Philosophy, University of Helsinki, 1976, p. 1.

[3] Boethius, Commentarii in Librum Aristotelis Περὶ Ἑρμενείας, editio secunda, C. Meiser, Teubner, Leipzig, 1877, p. 234.

the necessity at time *t* of the state that *p* means that it is true at *t* and at any time after that that *p* or, considering the atemporal nature of truth,[4] that it is true that *p* at *t* and any later time—in symbols $N_t p =_{df} (t')(t \leqslant t' \rightarrow p_{t'})$. Accepting the received view of how the modal notions are inter-related, it follows from this definition that it is possible at *t* that *p* if, and only if, at *t* or some later time, it is true that *p*. In symbols: $M_t p =_{df} (Et')(t \leqslant t' \& p_{t'})$.

III

The idea that, if *p* at *t*, then it is necessary, at *t*, that *p* at *t* must be distinguished from the idea that, if *p* at *t*, then it is necessary that it should have been or have come to be the case that *p* at *t*. The second is an idea about "determinism". Aristotle himself was anxious to distinguish it from the idea that that which is is necessary when it is. He was not, at least did not wish to be, a determinist. "It is clear (φανερὸν ἄρα), he says (19a18–19), "that not everything is or takes place of necessity" (ὅτι οὐχ ἅπαντα ἐξ ἀνάγκης οὔτ' ἔστιν οὔτε γίνεται). But to the question what it is to be or to take place (come to be, happen) of necessity (ἐξ ἀνάγκης) Aristotle has, I think, no very clear answer.

One way of understanding the determinist idea would be the following: if it is of necessity the case that *p* at *t*, then it was (already) before *t* necessary that it should be the case that *p* at *t*. It was, as one would naturally express oneself, *predetermined* or *antecedently necessary* that *p* at *t*. Universal determinism would then imply that *everything* "which is or takes place" is predetermined.

This notion of antecedent necessity is what I propose to call a *diachronic modality*. We already have (see above p. 61) the means for expressing the notion in symbols. "$N_{t'}p_t \& t' < t$" says that it is necessary at time *t'* that *p* at the later time *t*. It says in other words that the truth that *p* at *t* is predetermined at *t'* or from *t'* onwards. That a truth is antecedently necessary from a certain time onwards does not entail logically that it was predetermined from *any* earlier time or "from the dawn of creation".

On this view, determinism is an idea of diachronic necessity (modality)—and the Aristotelian thesis which we are now discussing an idea of *synchronic* necessity (modality). (The notions of diachronic and synchronic modalities will be further discussed in a later essay in this collection.)

---

[4] Cf. above, the essay "Determinism and Future Truth", pp. 5f.

IV

How then shall one understand the idea that that which is is necessary when it is—if this means neither that it is necessary *simpliciter* nor that it is or has come to be "of necessity" (is predetermined)?

In order to place the question in a new perspective we shall, for a moment, return to Diodorus.

Diodorus was famous not only for his "statistical" view of modality, mentioned earlier (Section II), but chiefly for his so-called κυριεύων or Master Argument. What exactly this was is obscure, but one way of characterizing it is to say that it was an attempt to *prove*, independently of Diodorus's "definition" of possibility mentioned above (p. 74), that if something is possible then it either is (already) or will be (in future) true. In symbols we can express this by $M_t p \rightarrow (Et')(t \leqslant t' \& p_{t'})$. Innumerable attempts have been made, not least in the past few decades, to capture or reconstruct the "proof" which Diodorus seemed to have thought ended in this conclusion. I shall not here attempt another reconstruction.[5] But mention should be made of one of the premisses which played a role in Diodorus's reasoning.

This premiss says that everything which is past and true is also necessary: πᾶν παρεληλυθὸς ἀληθὲς ἀναγκαῖον εἶναι.

How shall we understand this? Evidently not as saying that only things which are necessary *simpliciter* have been true in the past. Nor as saying that everything which was or came to be true was or did this "of necessity", was predetermined. If this were its meaning, the thesis would be pointless or uninteresting unless applied also to all *future* truths. As it stands, the thesis should be taken as compatible with some past truths being necessary *simpliciter*, others again being predetermined, and still others being contingent and not "of necessity". This third alternative Diodorus, who is reported to have been a determinist, might have wanted to dispute—but not on the basis of the premiss alone that past truths are necessary.

Did Aristotle, too, subscribe to the thesis about *the necessity of the past*, as I shall call it? Maybe he did, or would have done so—but I have not found any *clear* statement to this effect in his writings.

If it is maintained that everything which is past and true is necessary, it is pertinent to ask "*When* necessary?". And the answer seems obvious:

---

[5] I have tried to give one in my paper "The 'Master Argument' of Diodorus", in *Essays in Honour of Jaakko Hintikka*, ed. by E. Saarinen, R. Hilpinen, I. Niiniluoto, and M. Provence Hintikka, D. Reidel, Dordrecht, 1979, pp. 297–307.

necessary *after* it was or came to be true. The necessity is, so to say, there "in retrospect". It is thus, like the necessity of the predetermined, a *diachronic* necessity (modality). We could express the Diodorean idea in symbols as follows: $p_t \rightarrow (t')(t < t' \rightarrow N_{t'}p_t)$. This is then asserted to hold for all values of "p" and "t".

In the way the thesis of the necessity of the past is here understood it thus says that every *fait accompli*, i.e. everything which is or has come true at a certain time, is *thereafter* also necessary.

V

After this digression we return to the Aristotelian thesis on the necessity of the present. Does not the idea of the necessity of the past apply to the present, too, when understood as I do here? Surely everything which is now is a *fait accompli* as much as everything which was in the past. If by the past we mean everything which *already* is or has come true, we must classify the now with the past. What now is, already belongs, as a limiting point, to "history".

If in our symbolic expression for the thesis on the necessity of the past we replace the sign < by ⩽ we get $p_t \rightarrow (t')(t \leqslant t' \rightarrow N_{t'}p_t)$. Then the Aristotelian thesis in our symbolic formulation $p_t \rightarrow N_t p_t$ becomes derivable as a limiting case of the Diodorean thesis.

This is how we shall understand it here. But let it also be said that I do not claim that this is the only (interesting) way in which this thesis can be interpreted. Nor do I claim that this is how Aristotle understood it (cf. above p. 72). The double thesis of the necessity of the past *and* the present I shall call the thesis of *the necessity of the factual*.

VI

The thesis about the necessity of the factual, as I here understand it, is related to an important *asymmetry* between that which has already come to be and that which is yet to come. This asymmetry, furthermore, has to do with that which *we* call *causality*. (The emphasis on "we" alludes to the fact that the category of causality with Aristotle and the Aristotelian tradition may seem to us alien. What we think of as causes or causal conditions have, mainly at least, to do with the ways things come to be or originate. Such causes are of the kind which, in the Aristotelian tradition, have become known as efficient causes—as distinct from material, formal, and essential causes.)

The future, we think, "causally depends", partly if not in every detail, on the past. What has come to be, happened, often "conditions" or "determines" something which is, or is not, going to happen. The fact that something or other occurs first can, as we say, "make a difference" to what will occur later. For this reason we can sometimes *by doing things* influence what is going to be: *prevent* something which would otherwise happen, or *produce* something which otherwise would not come to be.

None of these causal (conditioning) relations hold in the reverse direction. What has been is not "influenced", we think, by what comes later. The fact that something or other occurs later cannot "make a difference" to what has occurred earlier. Therefore it is not possible for anything future to *prevent* anything from otherwise having happened or to *produce* something which is already there. (But past things can take on a *new significance* because of later events—perhaps because of the way in which those past things themselves contributed causally to "making a difference" to that which followed later.)

Such thoughts as these are sometimes expressed by saying that the past is "closed", the future "open". But this is only a metaphor. A more direct way of conveying the idea is to say, with Aristotle,[6] that potentialities are for the present or future.

Speaking in terms of efficient causality, one could say that the causal relation is asymmetrical and holds "in the direction of time".

But all these sayings, about asymmetry or causal dependence or potentiality, need clarification before we can claim fully to understand them. And not until we understand them can we judge whether they are true.

VII

Before proceeding we must do away with a possible misunderstanding. Does not the idea of the necessity of the past and the present, when interpreted as we do it here, amount simply to saying that facts cannot be changed, history not "erased", things done not undone? If this were the case, then the idea which Aristotle expressed in the sentence under discussion from the ninth chapter in *De Interpretatione* would be essentially the same as the one to which he gives expression when discussing deliberation in *Ethica Nicomakhea* 1139b10–11, quoting the words of the poet Agathos:

> μόνου γὰρ αὐτοῦ καὶ θεὸς στερίσκεται. ἀγένητα ποιεῖν ἅσσ' ἂν ᾖ πεπραγμένα.
> ("This only is denied even to God, to make what has been done undone.")

---

[6]*De Caelo* 283b13.

If this is how we have to understand the idea of the necessity of the past and present, the idea would be a mere triviality.[7]

The past and present cannot be changed. But why? The idea that it "might" be changed rests on a misconception of the notion of *change*. Change is not the substitution of some "*q*" for some "*p*" such that, whereas before *p* (was) at *t*, now *q* (is) at *t*. Change is a *progression in time*—from something which was at a certain time to something else which is at a different time.

What was was: this cannot be changed. But that holds equally for the future. *Que sera sera* can also express the same trivial truth. Tomorrow there will be a sea battle or there will not be a sea battle and nothing can "change" the alternative which (actually) comes true to its contradictory for tomorrow—nor, for that matter, "prevent" the alternative which actually comes true from having come true. And this in no way implies that one may not be able to prevent the one alternative or the other from coming true.

Facts—whether past, present, or future—cannot change (and therefore cannot be changed either). This is at bottom but another way of affirming the *atemporality* of the notion of truth. To say that it is true at t_1 but not at t_2 that *p* at *t* is sheer confusion and nonsense.

VIII

Let us assume that it is true that *p* at *t* and that we say: if it had not been the case that *q* at *t'*, it would not have been the case that *p* at *t* either, where *t'* is earlier than *t*. We often say things like that, and think we have good reasons for holding them true. We say, for example: "If it had not been raining during the night, the lawn would not have been so wet in the morning."

In saying things like this it seems to be presupposed that it need not have been the case that *q* at *t'*. If, therefore, we could have *made* it so that this had not been the case, then we could also have *prevented* that *p* at *t* from having been the case. And if neither we nor anybody else could have prevented this, then—as the locution goes—the "circumstances" might have been such that it would not have been true that *q* at *t'* and therewith also not that *p* at *t*. *We* could not have prevented the rain from falling, but if, for example, the wind had moved the clouds in a different direction it would not have rained in the night and the lawn would not have been (so) wet. And we believe that the weather conditions *could* have been dif-

[7]Cf. W. and M. Kneale, *The Development of Logic*, Oxford, 1962, p. 119.

ferent. I cannot see myself how we could assert and claim it to be true that whether it is or is not the case that p at t *depends on* whether it is the case or not that q at t', unless this last, *viz.* that q at t', is, in some sense, *contingent*, i.e. something which although it was the case might not have been the case.

In the case, as we have presented it, the fact that it is true that q at t' was a (*causally*) *necessary condition* of the fact that it is true that p at t. From this it follows that it would have been a (causally) sufficient condition of it not having been the case that p at t that it had not been the case that q at t'. If, in other words, one had prevented it from being the case that q at t' one would therewith also have prevented it from being the case that p at t.

Let us now look at the case in the reversed perspective of time. t' comes after t. "p_t" might, for example, be "it is raining at t", and "$q_{t'}$" be "the lawn is wet at t'".

Is it conceivable that, whether p at t, now *depends upon* whether q at t'?

Assume that we do not know whether it has been raining during the night. We step out into the garden to see whether the lawn is wet. If it is *not*, we say: "It cannot have been raining because then the lawn would be wet." If again the lawn *is* wet, we say perhaps: "It must have been raining". Or, counting also with the possibility that someone might have watered the lawn: "It might have rained."

Observing whether the lawn is wet in the morning can be a way of ascertaining whether it has been raining during the night. It may even, depending upon the circumstances, be our only way of ascertaining this. Ascertaining it presupposes that that p at t is a (*causally*) *sufficient condition* of that q at t' and that q at t', accordingly, a (causally) necessary condition of that p at t. That, from the fact that the lawn is dry, one can infer that it has not been raining depends upon (presupposes) that if it had been raining the lawn would be wet.

In order, however, to be able to maintain of something (that p) which was at t that it depended causally upon that something else (that q) took place at later time t', one would have to think that, if that q had not been at t', this would have prevented that p from having been at t. Why is this absurd?

If it not being the case that q at t' prevents that p at t, then that q at t' is a necessary condition of that p at t. And if this is the case then also that p at t is a sufficient condition of that q at t'. But if it is true that p at t and that p at t is a sufficient condition of that q at t', then nothing which is or happens *between* t and t' can prevent that q from being the case at t'. This can only be prevented by something which occurs *before* t and which would also have prevented that p from having been the case at t.

The notion of preventing, one could say, is *essentially anticipatory*. *Pre*-venting, *fore*-stalling means that something which (otherwise) would have been or happened at a certain time, was made impossible ("made impossible" in the sense of "was prevented") by something which occurred *before* this time or, possibly, at this very time but not later.[8] This is why that which is or was could not have been prevented by something which might have occurred (but did not occur) later—whereas that which is or was might not have been had something, which did not occur, occurred earlier.

IX

The two basic forms of causal efficacy are *prevention* and *production*. That which produces something else is a *sufficient* condition of it; therefore the existence of the thing produced is a *necessary* condition of the existence of the producing factor.

When causal efficacy with regard to states of affairs is concerned, production and prevention are interdefinable. To produce a state is to prevent its contradictory from obtaining—and to prevent a state from obtaining is to produce its contradictory.

If something is a sufficient condition of something else, the latter is a necessary condition of the former. This is so independently of how the two things are temporally related. If rainfall is a sufficient condition of the lawn becoming wet, then the lawn being wet is a necessary condition of rain having fallen. Rainfall is also causally efficacious in relation to wetting the lawn: it *wets* the lawn, *makes* it wet, *produces* wetness on the lawn. But wetting the lawn is *not* causally efficacious in relation to rainfall: by keeping the lawn dry one could *not* have *prevented* rain from falling. If there is a certain awkwardness or hesitation in calling the lawn's being wet a necessary condition of rainfall this, presumably, is due to a tendency to identify conditionship with causal efficacy. A conditionship relation is symmetrical in the sense that its terms are conditions of one another, whereas a relation of causal efficacy or dependence is asymmetrical.

It had been raining and the lawn became wet. Why can we not make the fact that the lawn was wet in the morning "responsible" for the rainfall during the night?

---

[8]The existence of "simultaneous causation" is problematic. Cf. my discussion of the problem in *Causality and Determinism*, Columbia University Press, New York, 1974, pp. 62–8. See also below, pp. 127ff.

I think the answer is that production, like prevention, is essentially "anticipatory" or "forward-looking". To produce is to bring about something which *is not yet*. Therefore that which *already* is or has been cannot have been produced by anything which comes later.

X

That which of necessity is or happens cannot be prevented. Therefore, *in a sense*, the fact that nothing which was could not have been prevented by anything which might have been later makes the past and present necessary in relation to what follows after. This is how I wish to understand the *dicta* of Diodorus and of Aristotle.

The core of my argument why nothing later can "make a difference" to anything earlier is the idea that "a direction of time" is built into our notions of preventing and producing. It is characteristic of the logical "grammar" of these notions, one could say, that they are "forward-looking". Therefore nothing can affect (causally) that which already is factual, a *fait accompli*. In relation to that which is still to come, the factual is like something necessary.

But are we not being dogmatic? *Must* preventing and producing be forward-looking? If saying that they are is making a "grammatical remark", could we not change our grammar, or at least imagine it changed, and therewith also reverse the direction of causation?

Some philosophers have entertained a, not always very well articulated, idea about *teleology* as "backward causation". Something which is necessary if a certain end is to be attained is then thought of as "caused", "brought forth", "produced" by that end. Is this sheer confusion, or superstition?

Suppose it is thought, or maybe is well established, that that p at t is an antecedent necessary condition of that q at t'. For example, some process in the brain in relation to movements of our limbs. Suppose, moreover, that we do not know, perhaps have not the faintest idea, of anything which might have occurred before t and produced that p. In relation to what was before, that p seems to us "causeless", "fortuitous", "spontaneous". Under certain circumstances it would then not be unnatural to say that had it not been for that q at t' it would not have been the case that p at t either, or that p at t, *because q* at t', or even—although this would surely sound provocative—that q at t' "produced" that p at t. The circumstances when this might be said would have to do with our familiarity with, or interest in, the phenomenon that q or with its "significance" to other things. But I shall not here investigate in detail the nature of these circumstances. Nor shall I pronounce on the question whether such an idea of "teleology as reversed causation" is worth entertaining or should rather be abandoned.

Note on Preventing and Producing

In the above discussion of causal efficacy we have been speaking of the *obtaining of states* of affairs ("that p at t") as being causally efficacious in relation to the obtaining of some other states of affairs ("that q at t'").

That something prevents it from being the case that p at t means that without this "something"—I shall speak of it as the preventive factor—it would be the case that p at t but with (because of) it it is not the case that p at t. This covers two different cases. One is when it is the case (immediately) before t that not-p and the preventive factor "forces" this state of affairs to continue (at t). The other is when it is already the case that p (immediately) before t but the preventive factor "forces" the prevailing state of affairs to vanish (at t). In the first case, a state is prevented from *coming* to be—in the second, something is prevented from *continuing* to be. The first case may also be spoken of as a case of *suppressing* a state, and the second as a case of *destroying* a state. In the first case one can also say that what is *prevented* is, strictly speaking, not a state but a *change*. It seems to me useful for the sake of conceptual clarity to reserve the term "prevent" for (the prevention of) changes, and not use it for the case when a state is prevented from continuing. In this latter case I shall not use the term "prevent" but speak either of destroying a state which is or, which means the same, *producing* the contradictory (negation) of a state which is not (yet).

With these terminological conventions, the two forms of causal efficacy which we distinguished (above, p. 80) *viz.* the preventive – suppressive and the productive–destructive forms, are *not* interdefinable. The exercise of causal interference which is preventive (suppressive) *results* in a not-change in a situation in which "otherwise", i.e. had it not been for the existence of a preventive factor, a change would have taken place. The exercise of causal interference which is productive (destructive) results in a change.

A change can be defined as a transformation or transition between states of affairs.[1] First a certain state obtains, and then the contradictory of that state. I shall use the symbol "$pT \sim p$" for the change which takes place when the state that p vanishes, i.e. passes out of existence or ceases to obtain, and "$\sim pTp$" for the opposite case when the state that p comes

---

[1] Cf. *Norm and Action*, Routledge & Kegan Paul, London, 1963, p. 27ff.

to be. "*pTp*" then signifies that the state in question does not change, continues to obtain, and " ~ *pT* ~ *p*" that it continues to be absent.

I shall not here make any specific assumption concerning the "time of change", for example, that changes are instantaneous or that there is a "period of transition" during which the changing state does *no longer* obtain but its contradictory state does *not yet* obtain. (Cf. above pp. 36ff. on "dialectical synthesis".) That one change takes place immediately before another change could be symbolized, e.g., by " ~ *pT* (*p* & ~ *qTq*)".

The causal efficacy of a change or not-change in relation to another change or not-change is normally restricted to a frame of "prevailing circumstances" *C*. A change which under certain circumstances may prevent another change from taking place, may under different circumstances not have this power. *C* often has an "open" character, meaning that we do not (or cannot) tell exactly of what states, changes, and not-changes *C* is composed. Problems about the composition and specification of *C* will not concern us here. (See below, pp. 139ff.), for a discussion of these questions.)

Let us now look a little closer into the logical structure of prevention. A change ~ *qTq* prevented another change ~ *pTp* from occurring. This means that the occurrence of ~ *qTq* was, under the circumstances, sufficient to make ~ *pTp not* occur, i.e. to warrant the constancy ~ *pT* ~ *p*. It does not mean that ~ *qTq* was also necessary for this end. Some other change, say ~ *rTr* which did not take place on that occasion but might also have taken place, could have the same preventive power. But if ~ *pTp* was *prevented*—and not only just did not occur—*some* such preventive change must have occurred then. This is necessary. Moreover, it is also necessary that, had it not been for the prevention, the change ~ *pTp would have* occurred. And this normally presupposes that something else was present or did occur on the occasion under consideration which is such that it would have *produced* the change ~ *pTp* then had none of the preventive changes occurred. It is natural, maybe even compelling, to think of that productive "something" as another *change,* say ~ *sTs*, with the power of producing the change ~ *pTp* under circumstances which satisfy at least these two conditions: (1) the state that *p* is initially absent and (2) the initial states of the preventive changes remain present.

When I said above that the prevented change "normally" has a cause I was thinking of the following possibility: could it not be that, had it not been for the preventive change, the prevented change would have occurred, but *causelessly*? This certainly is a possibility; only a dogmatic determinist would deny it. And if ~ *pTp* would have occurred without a cause, had some of the changes ~ *qTq*, ~ *rTr*, etc. not occurred, it is probably right to say that the occurrence of one of these latter changes "prevented"

$\sim pTp$ from occurring. But since the imagined possibility is contrary to fact, could we ever have any reason for thinking that $\sim pTp$ would have occurred causelessly on an occasion when it did not, in fact, occur? I think the answer is No. Whereas we are all familiar with situations in which it is practically certain that a change $\sim pTp$ would have occurred unless prevented, because of the presence of a (familiar) cause for its occurrence.

The occurrence of the change $\sim qTq$ prevented the change $\sim pTp$ from occurring, we say. Would we then also say that the change $\sim qTq$ was a cause of the non-change $\sim pT \sim p$? It would of course be quite in order to say that $\sim pTp$ did not occur *because* $\sim qTq$ occurred. This is merely another way of saying that the second change prevented the first. But to call the second change a cause of the constancy $\sim pT \sim p$ strikes me as not very natural.

By "corresponding" changes and not-changes we shall mean two changes with the same initial state and contradictorily opposed end-states, for example $\sim pTp$ and $\sim pT \sim p$. Although a preventive change is not naturally spoken of as a *cause* of the not-change corresponding to the prevented change, it is commonly and naturally spoken of as a *counteracting cause*. By calling it "counteracting" one then means that the preventive change, say $\sim qTq$, made inoperative (and in this sense "prevented") a cause of the prevented change, let it be $\sim pTp$, which was there and would have produced $\sim pTp$ had it not been for the prevention.

Assume that in order that a change should occur in the state that $\sim p$ it is required that another state, that $\sim q$, changes. We think, for whatever reason, that the change $\sim pTp$ will not occur *without a cause* (then) and that its *only cause* (either in general or under the circumstances) is the change $\sim qTq$. But the state that q continues absent and, as a consequence, the state that p too. Would one then say that the constancy or not-change $\sim qT \sim q$ *prevented* the state that $\sim p$ from changing? As far as I can see, one would never say this. The change $\sim qTq$ did not occur and therefore another change $\sim pTp$ did not occur either, a change, moreover, which would have occurred, had the first change occurred. But this, by itself, does not mean that $\sim pTp$ was prevented. It would have been prevented only if, under those circumstances, something had *prevented* $\sim qTq$ from occurring—say the occurrence of a further change $\sim rTr$. This further change, one would then say, "kept" the state that $\sim q$ constant and thereby prevented the state that $\sim p$ from changing.

A change can not be prevented (merely) by a not-change. Only a change can prevent a change.

We next turn our attention to productive causal efficacy. Whereas prevention results in not-change, production results in change, we have said. The productive causal relation is assumed to hold within a frame of prevailing circumstances C.

Assume that both $\sim qTq$ and $\sim rTr$ but no other change under those circumstances can produce the change $\sim pTp$. The change $\sim qTq$ occurs, and consequently $\sim pTp$. The occurrence of the first change was sufficient for the production of $\sim pTp$ and so would the occurrence of the second change have been. If both happened to occur we cannot "attribute" the productive effect more to the one than to the other of the two changes. No factor can be singled out as *the* cause of the resulting change—but this does not mean that the change occurred without cause. Its occurrence was, on the contrary, *overdetermined* as one would say.

The fact that there are only those two changes which can *produce* the change $\sim pTp$ does not exclude the possibility, however, that the change in question *takes place* (happens, occurs) also when neither $\sim qTq$ nor $\sim rTr$ takes place. Because something can take place also without being produced, *viz.* if this thing happens, as we would say, causelessly, without any cause. Only if *determinism* reigns is this excluded. One of the many meanings of "determinism" is precisely this: that everything which happens has at least one antecedent causal sufficient condition *and* that the disjunction of all its antecedent causal sufficient conditions is a necessary condition of it.[10]

Just as the fact that something comes to be does not logically entail that it has been *produced*, the fact that something remains as it is does not entail that it has been *prevented* (from changing). To think that everything which does not change is causally "forced" not to change, i.e. is prevented, would be to assume a very much stronger form of determinism than that form which only requires that every *change* is caused. The distinction between these two ideas of determinism reflects an *asymmetry* in our notions of producing and preventing.

Assume, finally, that there are two states such that if the first remains absent, $\sim qT \sim q$, or the second present, rTr, then a third state will come to be, $\sim pTp$. The first remains absent, and the third comes to be. That the first state remained absent was, under the circumstances, a sufficient condition for making the third state originate. This does not mean, however, that the constancy $\sim qT \sim q$ was a "cause" of the change $\sim pTp$. The cause, presumably, was some other change which took place then, and which has the power of producing the change $\sim pTp$ on condition, however, that the prevailing circumstances do not change in the absence of the state that q and presence of the state that r.[11]

---

[10]Cf. my book *A Treatise on Induction and Probability,* Routledge & Kegan Paul, London, 1951, pp. 72–4 and 131–35.

[11] For further considerations about the causal relations between changes and not-changes, and about the notion of a cause, see my book *Causality and Determinism,* Columbia University Press, New York, 1974, pp. 70–9.

On Causal Knowledge

I

Let us first consider an example of knowledge "based on induction", which is *not* causal. The example shall be that ravens are black. What does a man intimate (imply) about himself, if he says that he *knows* that ravens are black?

I think most of us, educated persons, would say that we know this. Would we also say we know that *all* ravens are black? I think we should feel hesitant to stress the "all". This, I think, is significant. Saying that we know that ravens are black is not to say, by implication, that we know that there will never, never be an exception to a certain "uniformity of nature".

Why would we say we know that ravens are black? How many ravens have we seen? Most of us very few, if any. We have seen pictures of ravens; we have read about ravens in zoology books; we are familiar with what may be called the "proverbial" blackness of ravens. This is "second-hand" knowledge. At the basis of it is, of course, long familiarity with a species of birds the members of which invariably (or nearly so) have been found to be black. A member of the species would normally be identified on the basis of a few characteristics, of which blackness is one. "Are you sure the bird you saw was a raven?" "Yes, it was quite black, this big, and sitting on a carcass." If raven-like but not-black birds are observed, we might lay these cases aside as "exceptions". Perhaps a zoologist or an experienced man in the woods could explain them to us. Single cases of this kind would not affect man's common knowledge that ravens are black. If there occurred markedly many of them in, say, a hitherto little explored region of the world, we might have found a new species. Why could there not exist white ravens, since we know there are black swans?

Knowledge that ravens are black is part of our common, inherited knowledge. Knowledge that *all* ravens are black is not.

If the colour is one of the characteristics by which we identify birds as ravens, does this not mean that blackness is logically connected with ravenness? And, if so, then surely *all* ravens are black.

But who would insist that blackness is a defining characteristic of ravens (or of ravens in such and such parts of the world)? At most a philosopher, who wishes to maintain that the reason why we *know* that ravens are black is that blackness is conceptually tied to ravenness. He would be wrong, however. An ornithologist, I think, would not insist on a conceptual tie here.

For some purposes, however, blackness could be *made* a defining characteristic of ravens. This could be some practical, transient purpose—such as counting the number of live ravens in a district. Or it could be some scientific purpose—such as creating a taxonomy. (But even given such purposes as those mentioned one would, presumably, be willing to admit "exceptions".)

So, on what does our knowledge that ravens are black rest? Basically, of course, on extensive experiential data about the colour of (members of) a certain species of bird. But also on such facts as the following: (a) The absence of specific reasons for doubting the universal truth of the blackness of ravens. We have, for example, no reason to think that in a certain unexplored region there exist non-black ravens. (b) The fact that we have some idea of how to cope with apparent counterinstances. Non-black ravens might be albinos, or they might belong to a different species from the ravens with which we have been familiar.

II

Let us now consider causal knowledge. A primitive example of causal knowledge is that if I put my hand in the fire, it will hurt. Or that water in a kettle will start boiling if heated to a certain temperature.

These are things we *know*. But are they not too "primitive" and also too vague to be of much interest? What if for the second item of knowledge we substituted that pure alcohol boils when heated to 80°C? Or that water boils when heated to 100°C under normal atmospheric pressure (but not on the top of Mount Everest)? If the substituted items are said to be known, the question becomes relevant: Known to *whom*? To most people such items are only secondhand knowledge. (Also to most scientists.) But practically everyone of us has firsthand knowledge of the effects of heating a kettle of water on the stove.

Should we say that *what* every one of us knows is that water under normal pressure boils at 100°C, although not too many of us know that *this* is what he knows, i.e. that this is the "exact" expression of the content of his knowledge?

This would not be right. The "common knowledge" that water boils, if heated, is not confined to situations when normal pressure obtains. It is therefore not "implicitly" knowledge that water boils if heated to a certain temperature, either. But neither is it unrestrictedly knowledge that "water boils when heated". It is common experience that if the flame under the kettle is weak and—as a person with rudimentary knowledge of physics would say—a loss of heat to the surroundings from the kettle and the water takes place, then even prolonged heating may not result in boiling. So, the efficiency of the heating must not be "off-set" by prevailing circumstances and ongoing processes.

What then is it that we *know* about heating water and making it boil? In the individual case, we are absolutely certain that the water in the kettle which I placed on the stove will start boiling in a few minutes' time. This is what water under such circumstances does when there is fire under the kettle. We *know* this.

We know that, under certain circumstances, water boils when heated. We could not describe these circumstances in detail, but in the individual case we can normally tell with certainty whether they obtain.

I think this is how we should describe the epistemic situation. It seems that there is thus a "double knowledge" involved. There is knowledge of a generality, a "uniformity of nature". And there is a certainty, in the individual case, that the circumstances are such that this uniformity will manifest itself.

Why is it that it seems more appropriate to call our grasp of the concrete situation "certainty" rather than "knowledge"? This is not an idle question. Let us ask: What is it that we know about the individual situation which makes us sure that, if we light the stove and put a kettle of water on it, the water will within a couple of minutes start boiling? It seems that *nothing in particular* which we know about the situation is of relevance to this certainty. Relevant is rather the fact that we do *not* know anything about the situation which would make us think that, maybe, heating will not now be efficient in making the water boil. Our confidence in the working of the causal law on this particular occasion rests on the *absence* of reasons for thinking the contrary. We *know* that the law has worked on countless occasions in the past; we also know of occasions when the law did not work and have at least a rough idea how to characterize them; we have no reason to think that *this* occasion is "exceptional" rather than "normal"; *therefore* we are certain that the law will work here.

III

The physicist's knowledge that, at normal pressure, water boils at 100°C is not causal knowledge in the first instance, but logical knowledge based upon a convention fixing the centigrade scale. But "behind" this convention there is substantive knowledge about natural regularities—and at the very bottom there is our primitive causal knowledge that water can be made to boil by heating it.

Consider, however, some other liquid, the boiling-point of which is not by convention connected with a degree on the thermometer, but which is genuinely "measured". *Spiritus fortis*, at normal pressure, boils at approximately 80°C. *I* know this from books on chemistry. How do chemists know it? Most of them from books, I presume. But some have made experiments. Perhaps this was in the course of their training. Then the experiments were not undertaken for the sake of checking or confirming the law—but rather for the sake of teaching the student experimental techniques. Deviant results would have shown that the circumstances had not been kept under the required control—not that the boiling-point of the liquid was, after all, *not* what the books say. But, of course, at the very basis of the knowledge which the chemistry books transmit, there are carefully conducted experiments undertaken in order to find out the boiling-point. I have no idea how many such experiments have been made. Perhaps in the case of some liquids, *one* was sufficient.

"Under" the chemists' and physicists' knowledge about the boiling- and melting-points of various stuffs, there is a mass of prescientific knowledge to the effect that each stuff changes its state of aggregation under roughly similar conditions of temperature—and not now at one and on another, seemingly similar, occasion at a widely different temperature. And "surrounding" and "supporting" this knowledge is a body of scientific knowledge (about molecular compounds, atomic structure, etc.) which makes us expect, and partly explains, these facts about changes in states of aggregation. The fact that this supporting body consists of chemical and physical *theories* does not make the term "knowledge" inapplicable here.

We also have an idea when a claim to scientific knowledge can be *questioned*. New experimental techniques, for example, may enable us to determine boiling- and melting-points with still greater exactitude and thus to correct previous values. Experiments and observations under new conditions—say, extremely high or low pressures—may make us better aware of the restrictions to which observed regularities of nature are subject.

Questioning assumed scientific knowledge normally leads to "*improvements*" in our knowledge and not to "overthrow" of previous beliefs. This too we know. And this gives us a certainty that many of our present claims to scientific knowledge will never have to be completely renounced, but will at most become restricted relative to a bulk of old knowledge and old scientific techniques.

IV

Knowledge about boiling- and melting-points, whether scientific or prescientific, has the following characteristics which may be regarded as

typical of causal knowledge: First, it is knowledge of relationships between changes in nature, e.g. that a change in temperature will cause a
change in state of aggregation. Second, this knowledge is hypothetical in
the sense that it pertains to what will happen, *if* something else happens.
Third, it is relative to a frame of circumstances on the prevailing of which
we can normally rely in situations in which the causal relation is expected
to hold, or its validity is put to a test.

Knowledge such as, say, that ravens are black or, generally, about
typical features of members of a species and other "natural kinds" is different. It is not knowledge of how changes are related, but of how states
are correlated. It is thus in a characteristic sense *static* as distinct from
causal knowledge which is *dynamic*. Further, it is *categorical* and not
hypothetical. We know that there are ravens and that they are black. If
ravens become extinct this knowledge becomes "historical". We should
then know that there was a bird, the raven, of which a black colouring was
characteristic. If ravens were to change colour in future, we should know
that ravens used to be black. The fact that one can say truly "if this bird is
a raven, it is black" does not make knowledge that ravens are black
hypothetical. Ravens *are* black. So, *if* the bird you saw in the wood or
which was brought here for examination was not black, it probably
wasn't a raven. This illustrates one way in which a hypothetical can be
"hooked on" to our general knowledge about the colour of ravens.

V

The test of a causal uniformity requires that the circumstances under
which it is supposed to hold, are, somehow, within our control. For example: if we want to test that liquid X boils at Y degrees under normal
pressure, we must know how to test the pressure and preferably also how
to regulate it and keep it constant over the period of an experiment. We
must also have some control over the loss of heat from the liquid to the
instrument of measurement—know whether it has to be taken into account
or whether it is negligible. Controlling the circumstances thus presupposes
a great deal of "background" causal knowledge and skill to apply it in the
experimental situation. There is probably no testing of causal laws which
does not rely on causal knowledge (both scientific and prescientific). And
there is hardly any individual item of scientific causal knowledge which is
not "embedded" in a *system* of such knowledge.

VI

Our knowledge of a causal relation may have been obtained by successfully testing a *hypothesis*. It may also happen that a causal relation which was thought to be known later becomes subject to *doubt*.

A primitive or prescientific idea about a causal connection may become corrected with the advancement of (scientific) knowledge. There is (or was) a popular belief that being exposed to a cold temperature might cause a "cold". We now know that the symptoms of the illness are caused by bacteria—and that the cooling of the body is only a circumstantial condition under which the working of the bacteria on the body becomes "efficacious".

Getting cool/catching a cold is a very "rough" "uniformity of nature". Shall knowledge of it count as "causal knowledge" at all? What is here "common knowledge" is something like the following: under certain circumstances, letting oneself become cool easily results in a cold. If one had to characterize the circumstances in greater detail one could say, for example: when there is already a cold "about the place".

Suppose the circumstances are such that if a certain man exposes himself to a cold temperature, he will get a cold. (The germs are already in his body "awaiting an opportunity" to attack him.) He then gets cool—and a cold. Shall we say that the cooling, i.e. the drop in temperature of his body, was the cause of the cold? I think it is perfectly correct to say this.

But is this not to turn things upside down? Was not the "real" cause internal processes in the person's body, processes which in their turn were initiated by the germs? The drop in temperature was only a "condition" which, when it was satisfied, made the real cause "operative", i.e. productive of the malaise.

The distinction between "cause" and "condition" is familiar. And it is, for many purposes, a useful distinction to make. But what counts as condition and what as cause is not fixed "in the nature of things". The distinction is relative. Given the conditions under which a temperature-drop will make operative germs already present in the body, the temperature-drop is a cause and the presence of germs a condition. If, however, the germs are not yet in the body, but the conditions under which they would cause a cold are satisfied, then it is the infusion of germs which is the cause.

There may be reasons for calling the germs a "more real" cause of a cold than a drop in body-temperature: for example, that the germs can also be activated when no drop in temperature takes place, whereas a change in body-temperature cannot produce a cold unless there are germs. But this would not run contrary to the fact that there are circumstances under which it is perfectly correct (and not "unscientific") to say that a cold was caused by a drop in temperature of the body.

The reason for calling the temperature-drop "cause" should also be plain: it is the *change* which, under the circumstances, we hold responsible for another *change* (the "outbreak" of the cold). If, on another occasion, the cooling of the body does not result in a cold, we should say that the circumstances were not the "right" ones. For, we *know* that a temperature-drop *can* cause a cold, i.e. *will do* it under appropriate circumstances. This is "common knowledge".

VII

In an important type of case, to think that the happening of *c* is a cause of the happening of *e* commits one to holding that, "*ceteris paribus*", the happening of *c* will (always) be accompanied by the happening of *e*. Moreover, this "will be" is more than a statement about what will happen (*e*), *if* something else happens (*c*) under appropriate circumstances (*C*). In a characteristic sense, the "will be" also covers all "past futures" and all "future pasts". This means the following:

Of all past occasions when the circumstances *C* prevailed but *c* did not happen and of all future occasions when the circumstances *C* will have prevailed but *c* will not have happened, it is true that, *had c* been there on those occasions, *e would have* accompanied it.

It seems to me that it is in this implicit commitment to a counterfactual conditional assertion that our belief in the causal efficacy of one event upon another, or in the "causal bond" linking two events, consists.

If it is true that the differentiating mark between a causal bond and an accidental concomitance is that the former but not the latter supports counterfactual conditionals, then the question how one acquires causal knowledge is essentially the question how one can get to know, if at all, the truth of counterfactual conditionals.

Counterfactual conditionals are, one could say, *retrospective* statements. They speak about what would have happened, had something been different from what it actually was, is, or will have been. In the case of causal counterfactuals, the actuality is that, on some occasion or succession of occasions, the cause-event does not happen. The contrasting non-actuality is that both the cause- and the effect-event happen. In order to "verify" the counterfactual statement we ought somehow to make the actual and the non-actual "change place". How can this be done?

Literally this can of course not be done at all. Saying that the actual (factual) and non-actual (counter-factual) change place is a metaphor. But it may be a useful *façon de parler* in speaking about things which literally can and do take place.

As far as I can see, the acquisition of causal knowledge presupposes that there are situations in which we are *certain* that the cause- and the effect-events *will not* occur although they *can* occur. If the cause-event is something we can make happen, then, by producing it, we can actualize what otherwise would have remained unactualized. Assume now that in such a situation we make the cause-event happen. If, having done this, we find that the effect-event does not happen, we may conclude either that the presumed cause is not really a cause with that effect, or that the circumstances under which it is efficacious are not satisfied—or we may suspend judgement. If, however, we observe the effect-event we also know that, had the cause-event *not* occurred on that occasion, then it would have been true retrospectively to maintain that, *if* it had occurred, the effect-event would have accompanied it. We, as it were, "proved" this by making the cause-effect occur and observing what happened then. Metaphorically speaking, we proved it by making the actual and the non-actual "change place".

VIII

But could we not simply *wait* ("passively") for the cause-event to occur and then, when it occurs and is followed by the effect-event, gain the same insight into the counter-factual truth as we get from the "experiment"? I think the answer is "No." Mere observation of regular sequences in nature may suggest to us the existence of causal connections and may make us put forward various causal conjectures or hypotheses. Further observations may confirm or refute such hypotheses. Perhaps after long confirmation we say we "know" such a hypothesis to be true. It would be futile, I think, to dispute whether this can be genuine knowledge, or not. But it is important to see that and why the possibility of an experimentalist interference with the case changes the epistemic situation radically—not only in degree but in conceptual character. The following considerations should help us see this more clearly:

Suppose we are familiar from experience with a regular sequence: c_1 followed by c_2 followed by e. What sort of causal connectedness might this suggest? There are two possibilities. One is that c_1 causes c_2 which in turn causes e. The other is that c_1 is the cause of the sequence: c_2 followed by e. The problem connected with coming to know the second possibility is the same as the problem of coming to know a simple causal relation of the type: c causes e. The problem, again, of coming to know that there is a causal chain, c_1 causes c_2 which causes e is more complicated. It can be split up in two. The first is to come to know that c_1 causes the sequence: c_2 followed by e. On this we already commented. The second is to come to know that c_2, by itself, causes e. To this end we must study cases in which c_2 occurs, but *not* as an effect of c_1, nor of any other known cause of its occurrence. Because if the sequence c_2 followed by e is an effect of, say, c_1' then we are again faced with the problem of "detaching" c_2 from this cause in order to find out whether c_2, *by itself*, is causally efficacious. Thus in order to test the causal efficacy of c_2 there must exist, or we must by manipulation be able to secure the existence of, situations such that the introduction of c_2 into them is in our control, i.e. such that we are confident that c_2 and e will not make their appearance in them unless made to appear. If we can make and do make c_2 happen in such a situation and find that it is not followed by e, we may conclude that c_2 has not the causal power of producing e, at least not under the circumstances accompanying the experiment. If, again, e follows upon the appearance of c_2, we have confirmed that there is a causal connection between the two factors—as distinct from a mere concomitance due to the existence of a common cause for both of them. Because we are now entitled to say that had we let c_2 remain absent on the occasion when we made it happen, then it would have been true that *had* we made it happen, *e would have* followed. We "proved" this by intervening with that which we were certain would otherwise have taken place.

Our certainty *may*, of course, have been "deceptive" in the sense that the result of our intervention was, in fact, due to some cause external to us. But in order to find this out and come to regard this external factor as a cause of the sequence c_2 followed by e, we should again have to go through the same epistemic procedure for coming to hold another counterfactual conditional true.

Two very simple examples will illustrate these abstract lines of thought:

I put fire to a sheet of paper. The edge of the paper turns first brown then black, the sheet crumbles, and finally turns to ashes. The stages in this process are, broadly speaking, successive effects of *one* cause, viz. the heat (the flame) to which the paper is being exposed. It is not, for example, the change of colour at the edges which makes the paper crumble. How do I know this? Nothing is easier: I can give to a sheet of paper those successive colourings without producing the subsequent effects of the heat when it devours the sheet. And I can crumble the paper without turning it to ashes.

A stone hits a window and breaks it. Air enters the room from outside and there is a drop in indoor temperature. In this chain of events every link is a cause of the next one. It is not the hit of the stone against the glass which *first* breaks the window and *eventually* cools the room. It is the entering of outside air into the chamber which has the cooling effect. This is easily established—"experimentally" if needed.

IX

Our "common knowledge" of causes—such that water boils when

heated—is founded in man's accumulated experience about what follows (the effect) when a certain thing happens (the cause) under *familiar* circumstances. Such knowledge is often, perhaps usually, intimately interwoven with our practical life, i.e. with our ability to effect changes by doing other things under those circumstances—for example, to make water boil by heating it. When such a connection with manipulation is missing—as in the case of lightning and thunder, say—a conjectured causal connection is, at the prescientific stage, often associated with ideas of a being endowed with superhuman powers, for example a thunder-god. At a scientific stage, such conjectures are associated with a systematic search for experiments, i.e. for learning to *reproduce* the cause-event under *controlled* circumstances.

Why is it "irresistible" to think of lightning as the cause of thunder although the connection is not very similar to connections familiar from *our* practical life? This is worth reflecting about. I suppose that one reason is that lightning is a striking intervention with an existing state in nature. It is an event the (natural) *cause* of which is, at the prescientific stage, completely hidden from our knowledge. In this the occurrence of lightning resembles things the production of which is "in the hands" of an agent.

X

A cause, then, is something the occurrence of which *initiates* a sequence of events (also) when it is not itself the effect of another cause. The occurrence of a cause-event may of course be embedded in a *causal chain*, i.e. occur as the effect of another cause. But any later link in such a chain can be known to be (itself) causally efficacious only by being detached from the preceding links and made to occur as "initiator" of the succeeding part of the causal sequence.

If I am right in thinking that causal concatenations can be known only as detachable parts of bigger wholes within which non-caused initiation of changes is taken for granted, then the truth of *determinism* can at most become established for fragments of the world and not for the world as a totality. But may not determinism nevertheless be *true* for the totality—only we cannot come to *know* its truth? The question seems to me idle. How would this truth "manifest" itself? It manifests itself to the extent that we get to know causal connections between events of given generic character. *Belief* in determinism may influence our orientation in the world and direct our research. It can function as a constant urge to search for causes. But that determinism is true cannot itself be "causal knowledge".

Diachronic and Synchronic Modality

I

Let it be the case that p at t. The letter "p" here stands for a grammatically complete sentence which, however, does not express a true or false proposition unless it is qualified with respect to time. Such sentences are said to describe *generic* states of affairs.

Assume further that the fact that p at t is *contingent*. What does this mean? It seems natural to answer this question as follows: although it *is* the case that p at t it *need not* be so. But what this means is far from clear. Does it mean that it need not be so *then*? Using the letter "M" for "it is possible that", the suggestion is that the contingent truth that p at t is expressed in symbols by $p_t \mathbin{\&} M \sim p_t$.

This suggested answer to our question, however, is not unproblematic. Its problematic character is already reflected at the level of language. The strictly correct reading of $p_t \mathbin{\&} M \sim p_t$ is: "p at t and it is possible that (it is the case that) not p at t". The use of the present indicative in the bracketed clause sounds unnatural. A speaker of good English would say: "p at t but it might have been the case that not p at t".

II

I shall here suggest the following answer to our question what it means to say that it is *contingently true* that p at t: Some time t' before t it was (still) possible that the world would develop in such a way that, at t, it had been true that $\sim p$ and not that p. In symbols:

$$p_t \mathbin{\&} (Et')\,(t' < t \mathbin{\&} M_{t'} \sim p_t).$$

The idea is thus that the contingent truth of something presupposes the *antecedent possibility* of its contradictory. It is inviting to generalize this idea as follows: it is possible at a given time that something is true at that same time (regardless of whether it, as a matter of fact, is or is not true then) if, and only if, some time before it was antecedently possible that it would be true then. In symbols:

$$M_t p_t = (Et')\,(t' < t \mathbin{\&} M_{t'} p_t).$$

In this formula two kinds or types of modal attribution are involved. I shall say that "$M_t p_t$" expresses a *synchronic* modality meaning that the attribution of modal status is for the same time as the possible truth of the proposition to which the modal status is attributed. And I shall say that "$M_t p_t$" in the formula expresses a *diachronic* modality because of the temporal difference between the asserted validity of the attribution of modal status and the possible truth of the proposition whose modal status is involved.

The only kind of diachronic modality which will be considered here is when the attribution of modality is for a time anterior to the time of the truth or falsehood of the proposition to which modal status is attributed. Such attributions of modality might also be called *prospective* or forwardlooking. (Cf. below p. 118).

The identity-sign in the above formula ought to reflect the fact that we regard the formula as an attempt to "elucidate" the meaning of a synchronic attribution of modality in the terms of a diachronic attribution. The logical status itself of the elucidation I shall not discuss.

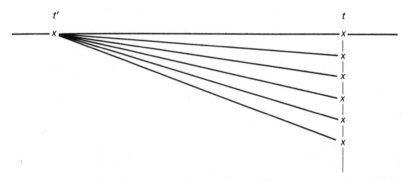

Figure 1

The things at *t* which are antecedently possible at *t′* can be spoken of as a "spectrum of possibilities", projected from (the world at) *t′* onto the "time-screen" at *t*. We can illustrate this in Figure 1. The points (*x*) at which the projective rays from *t′* hit the time-screen at *t* represent conjunctions of sentences, and/or their negations, which express true or false propositions when qualified with respect to time *t*. Such conjunctions describe (fragments of) various possible total states of the world at *t*. The points on the horizontal line represent the actual total state of the world at the given time.

III

If the proposition that *p* at *t* is true but not contingently so, then its contradictory is not possible. This, on the elucidation we gave, means that its contradictory is not *antecedently* possible. In symbols:

$$\sim M_t \sim p_t = \sim (Et')\,(t' < t \,\&\, M_{t'} \sim p_t).$$

Accepting the received view of the relation between possibility and necessity and shifting from the existential to the universal quantifier, the above formula may be rewritten as:

$$N_t p_t = (t')\,(t' < t \rightarrow N_{t'} p_t).^1$$

If it is true that $N_{t'}p_t$ then we shall say that it is *antecedently necessary* that p at t.

If a proposition is always antecedently necessary its truth will, moreover, be said to be *predetermined*. It is a convenient *façon de parler* to say that a proposition the truth of which is predetermined is necessary "from the beginning of the world (time)" or "from the dawn of creation".

IV

If it is *true*, whether contingently or necessarily, that p at t, then it is, trivially, also synchronically possible that p at t, i.e. $M_t p_t$. By its very actuality (existence) the truth of the proposition that p at t demonstrates, moreover, that it was *always* antecedently possible that p at t.

Assume now that at some time t' it is antecedently possible that p at t. Then, regardless of whether this proposition comes true or not at t, it must have been antecedently possible already at any time before t'. Because the actual state of the world at t proves by its existence that it was possible for the world to come to be in a state such that, at t, it might be true that p. Consequently, the projection from the actual state of the world at any time *before t'* onto the time-screen at t will yield a spectrum of possibilities which includes the proposition that p at t. It is therefore another convenient *façon de parler* to say that a proposition which is antecedently possible at a certain time was this (already) "at the beginning of the world".

We thus have $M_{t'}p_t \rightarrow (t'')\,(t'' < t' \rightarrow M_{t''}p_t)$. This formula, however, cannot be converted. Antecedent possibility *may*, but need not, "get lost". What this means can perhaps be best seen from an example:

---

[1] The meaning of "$N_t p_t$" when elucidated in this way must be distinguished from that other meaning of the expression "$N_t p_t$" given to it in the Aristotelian *dictum* on the necessity of that which is when it is. This second meaning too may be explained in diachronic terms, as a limiting case of the idea that what is true and past is necessary (see above, p. 76). Thus the meaning of the synchronic "$N_t p_t$" may be said to fall on the point where the prospective and the retrospective conceptions of diachronic modalities "meet".

A person is killed at *t* in an explosion. "Under the circumstances", we say, this was necessary—considering the strength of the explosion and that he happened to be near the exploding bomb. But he need not have been where he was at *t*. If at *t'* he had started to move away, which he could have done, he would not have been killed. But after *t"* this was too late. Even if he had started to run then, he would have been killed. At *t'* (and before) it was possible that he would be saved. But at *t"* (and after) this was no longer possible.

Since antecedent possibility may get lost, and since that which is antecedently possible at a certain time also was antecedently possible at any earlier time, it follows that the spectrum of possibilities on the time-screen at a certain time *t* *may* shrink and *cannot* widen when the point from which the projection is made approaches the state of the world at *t*. This is illustrated in Figure 2.

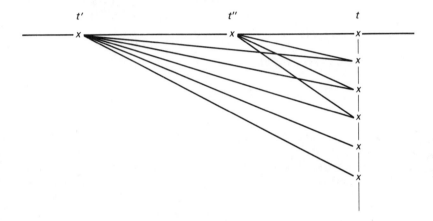

Figure 2

If the proposition that *p* at *t* at a certain point in time loses the antecedent possibility which it had before, then the proposition that *p* at *t* is, from that time on and up to time *t*, antecedently impossible—and its contradictory antecedently necessary. This kind of antecedent necessity, however, must be distinguished from the one we introduced earlier and called predetermination or antecedent necessity "from the beginning of the world". The second is a stronger notion (see below).

It follows from what was said about the sizes of spectra of antecedent possibility that antecedent necessity of a proposition, once it is acquired, cannot get lost. We thus have an entailment $N_{t'}p_t \rightarrow (t'') (t' \leqslant t'' \leqslant t \rightarrow N_{t''}p_t)$.

V

Let it be *necessarily* true that p at t. The meaning of such an attribution of modal status can be explicated in several ways. Here we are concerned only with its explication in the terms of antecedent necessity. It is readily seen, however, that there are two variants of such an explication:

That it is necessarily true that p at t can mean that the truth of this proposition is predetermined, antecedently necessary "from the beginning of the world". Or it can mean that its truth was antecedently necessary from a certain time t' before t (but not before t').

I shall say that the (synchronic) attribution of necessity to the proposition that p at t is *strong* or *weak* depending upon which of the two explications in the terms of antecedent necessity is contemplated. I shall also call antecedent necessity strong if it was always there, and weak if it was there from a certain time but not before. Thus we have for strong necessity the identity with which we are already familiar from Section III

$$N_t^s p_t = (t')\,(t' < t \rightarrow N_{t'} p_t),$$

and for weak necessity the identity

$$N_t^w p_t = (Et')\,(t' < t \,\&\, N_{t'} p_t).$$

VI

If it is *true*, whether contingently or necessarily, that p at t then this proposition has never lost the antecedent possibility which it had "at the beginning of the world". This is trivial. But also if it is *false* that p at t this proposition may never, before it turned out to be false, have lost its antecedent possibility of being true. (This last statement a determinist would deny.)

If the proposition that p at t was antecedently possible and never lost its antecedent possibility, then it will be said to be, at t, in the *strong* sense possible. If moreover, this proposition turns out false at t then it (and its contradictory) will be said to be in the *strong* sense contingent or "absolutely" contingent.

In contrast, the ideas of possibility and contingency which in Section II were explicated in terms of antecedent possibility, may be called *weak* possibility and contingency respectively. For weak possibility we have the identity

$$M_t^w p_t = (Et')\,(t' < t \,\&\, M_{t'} p_t),$$

and for strong possibility the identity

$$M_t^s p_t = (t')\,(t' < t \to M_{t'} p_t).$$

Let it be observed that the "dual" of weak possibility is strong necessity—and the "dual" of weak necessity is strong possibility.

One and the same proposition, say that p at t, may thus be both necessary and contingent. This means that it may be initially contingent but from a certain time before coming true necessary. What is in a longer perspective of time contingently true may yet in a shorter perspective be necessarily true. This is in good accord with the way we commonly talk and think about things which happen. I shall call (the truth of) a proposition which is initially contingent but "loses" its contingent character and "becomes" necessary (a) *contingently necessary* (truth) (see also above, p. 55 and below, p. 122.)

VII

The logic of the *synchronic* modalities is S5.

This is easily shown using the "time-screen" at t as a model. When the notion of weak (strong) possibility (necessity) is involved the model is composed of all "hits" on the screen from any point, however far, in the past. When strong (weak) possibility (necessity) is concerned the model retains only those hits which never get "blotted out" when the point of projection approaches the screen at t.

The hits on the screen represent alternative possible total states of the world at t. The description of such a total state will contain the conjunctive component "$M_t\,p_t$" if, and only if, at least one of the alternative descriptions contains "p_t". It follows that if "p_t" is a conjunctive component in *some* of the alternative descriptions, then it is a component in *all* of them. Conversely, if "p_t" occurs in none of the descriptions, then "$\sim p_t$" and *a fortiori* "$\sim M_t\,p_t$" occurs in *all* of them.

Assume next that "$M_t \sim M_t\,p_t$" is a conjunctive component in the description of the (actual) total state of the world at t. Then, by the above criterion, "$\sim M_t p_t$" will be a conjunctive component in at least one of the alternative descriptions. But by the same criterion "p_t" cannot occur in any of the descriptions, i.e. "$\sim p_t$" and hence also "$\sim M_t\,p_t$" will have to occur in them all. Herewith it has been shown that if it is true that $M_t \sim M_t p_t$, then it is also true that $\sim M_t\,p_t$.

For synchronic modality the reduction formula characteristic of S5 $M_t \sim M_t\,p_t \to\ \sim M_t\,p_t$ thus holds true.

VIII

Let $t' < t'' < t$.

"$M_{t'}\, p_t$" is a conjunctive component in the description of a possible total state of the world at t' if, and only if, "p_t" is a conjunctive component in the description of at least one possible total state of the world at t *within the spectrum of possibilities* projected from this state of the world at t' onto the time-screen at t.

It follows that "$M_{t'}M_{t''}p_t$" is a component in the description of a possible total state of the world at t' if, and only if, "$M_{t''}p_t$" is a component in the description of at least one possible state at t'' within the spectrum of possibilities projected from this state at t' onto the time-screen at t'' *and* "p_t" is a component of at least one possible state at t within the spectrum of possibilities projected from this state at t'' onto the time-screen at t. Since the second spectrum can at most coincide with, but may in fact be only a part of, the spectrum of possibilities projected from the state at t' onto the time-screen at t, it follows that "$M_{t'}p_t$" is a conjunctive component in the description of the total state of the world at t' in which "$M_{t'}M_{t''}p_t$" is a component. Figure 3—only the outer bounds of the spectra being marked by lines—illustrates this fact:

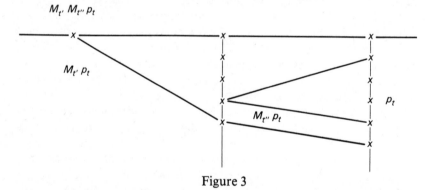

Figure 3

Herewith it has been shown that the reduction formula $M_{t'}M_{t''}p_t \rightarrow M_{t'}p_t$, characteristic of S4, holds for the notion of diachronic possibility.

It is easy to verify from the model that the reduction formula of S5 does *not* hold for the diachronic modalities. As shown by Figure 4, it may be possible at t' that it is impossible at t'' that it is the case that p at t, and yet be possible at t' that it is possible at t that p.

The above findings will suffice to support our statement that the logic of the (forward-looking or prospective) diachronic modalities is S4 (or is "S4-like").

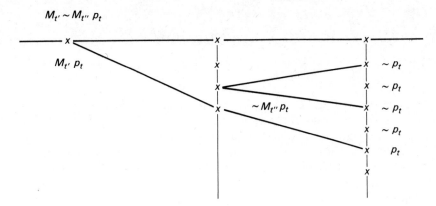

Figure 4

Logical Modality

I

The notions of diachronic and synchronic modality which were discussed in the preceding essay apply to individual instantiations (in time) of what elsewhere I have called *generic* propositions. That it is raining is a generic proposition—that it is raining at time *t* is an individual proposition, an instantiation at *t* of the generic proposition that it is raining. Generic propositions may also have instantiations in space, but the spatial component of individual propositions we shall leave out of consideration here.

Many generic propositions, for example the proposition that it is raining, have both true and false instantiations. It is sometimes raining, sometimes not raining. By an "instance" of a generic proposition I shall understand a *true* instantiation. Thus every case of rainfall constitutes an instance of the generic proposition that it is raining; one could also say that it is an instance of the generic state of rainfall. But *any* proposition that it is raining at *t* is an instantiation of the generic proposition that it is raining, irrespective of whether it is raining at *t* or not.

The modal notions in question were, moreover, temporal or temporalized. This was the ground for calling them "diachronic" and "synchronic". A proposition that *p* at *t* was pronounced possible or necessary *at a time t'* , different from or identical with *t*. Finally, we only considered the case when the diachronic modality was forward-looking or prospective.

Modal attributions also apply to generic propositions. Of the proposition that it is raining one would say that it is a contingent proposition (contingently true or false); the proposition that it is raining or not raining one would perhaps call necessary.

Since generic propositions are, "by themselves", neither true nor false it is appropriate to ask what it *means* to attribute modal status to them.

I shall here throughout assume that a generic proposition to which modal status is attributed, when instantiated yields propositions which *have* a truth-value, are either true or false. This assumption, it seems, must be made if attributions of modal status to generic propositions are to make sense at all.

There obviously exists some "bridge" between the attribution of modal status to generic and the attribution of truth-value to individual propositions. This much seems clear: if a generic proposition is necessary, then every instantiation of it is true. A necessary generic proposition, one could also say, is *universal*(ly true)—meaning that it has only true instantiations. Paying attention exclusively to temporal instantiations one could call the proposition *sempiternally* true (cf. above p. 7); counting also with spatial instantiations one sometimes says that such a proposition is true *semper et ubique*. An impossible generic proposition would then be universally false, not true in any instance.

II

Is the relation between necessity and universality reciprocal? Is a generic proposition which is universal also necessary?

In the *Principles of Mathematics* Bertrand Russell wrote: "there seems to be no true proposition of which there is any sense in saying that it might have been false".[1] And some fifteen years later he wrote in "The Philosophy of Logical Atomism": "Propositions can only be true or false. .... It is important, I think, to realize that the whole doctrine of modality only applies to propositional functions, not to propositions."[2]

Russell is here, in effect, denying that individual, true or false, propositions have modal status. Only generic propositions or—in Russell's terminology—propositional functions have such status. In his *Introduction to Mathematical Philosophy* he wrote: "If 'ϕx' is an undetermined value of a certain propositional function, it will be *necessary* if the function is always true, *possible* if it is sometimes true, and *impossible* if it is never true."[3] When this is read in conjunction with the quotation above from "The Philosophy of Logical Atomism" one feels confident that Russell understood the "if" in the sentence as an "if, and only if".[4]

In his famous essay "On the Notion of Cause" Russell, however, expressed himself a little differently. There he said: "A proposition is *necessary* with respect to a given constituent when it is the value, with that constituent as argument, of a necessary propositional function."[5] One could say that Russell here gives a meaning "by courtesy" to the modal status also of individual propositions—whereas in *The Principles of Mathematics* and "The Philosophy of Logical Atomism" he denies that

---

[1] Allen & Unwin, London, 1903, p. 454.

[2] Here quoted from *Logic and Knowledge*, ed. by R. Ch. Marsh, Macmillan, New York, 1956, p. 231.

[3] Allen & Unwin, London, 1919, p. 165.

[4] This is also the way Wittgenstein understood Russell's position when he criticized it in *Tractatus* 5.525. On Russell's view of possibility and its criticism by Wittgenstein, see also my book *Wittgenstein*, Basil Blackwell, Oxford, 1982, p. 189ff.

[5] *Proceedings of the Aristotelian Society,* **XIII** (1912–1913, p. 4.

true or false *propositions* can have modal status. Propositions are necessary, possible, or impossible in so far as they instantiate necessary, possible, or impossible propositional functions.

As seen from the definitions given, Russell endorsed a view according to which there is a reciprocal relation between necessity and universality. Not only is a generic proposition which is necessary universal, but the converse also holds good: if a generic proposition is universal, it is necessary. One could say that universality is a necessary and sufficient condition of necessity.

If this reciprocity between the two notions is accepted, an interesting consequence follows for the notion of possibility: a possible proposition cannot be sempiternally false. Because then it would be *im*possible. Hence it must have at least one true instantiation. The idea that everything possible sometimes comes true has been called the Principle of Plenitude. It has played a prominent role in the history of thought.[6]

When applied to generic propositions, the Principle of Plenitude entails acceptance of the definitional identities $Mp =_{df} (Et)p_t$ and $Np =_{df} (t)p_t$ or, alternatively, $Mp =_{df} \lor p$ and $Np =_{df} \land p$, where "$\lor$" is read "it is somtimes the case that" and "$\land$" is read "it is always the case that".

The view of modality which equates necessity with universality, and possibility with existence, encounters objections on intuitive grounds. This view appears to ignore a modal distinction "at a higher level" so to speak. Necessary truth of generic propositions is universal truth—let this be granted. But universal truth, it seems, can be either necessary or accidental (contingent). May it not *just so happen* that the generic proposition that p has only true instantiations, that it always is the case that p? And if this were to happen, would that be a sufficient ground for pronouncing the generic proposition necessary?

I think it is useful to check an impulse we may have to answer the last question off-hand in the negative. The notion of *accidental universal truth* is difficult to grasp. I can imagine that we, "finite" human beings, never encounter a false instantiation of a certain generic proposition—but is that "imagining" that it is universally true? I think not.

One cannot get round the difficulties by saying that the difference between necessary and accidental truth of universal generic propositions is that all instantiations of the latter are true in the *real* world, and all instantiations of the former also in every *possible* world. ("Necessary truth = truth in all possible worlds.") Because this is but another way of saying

---

[6] See the well-known work by Arthur O. Lovejoy, *The Great Chain of Being, A Study of the History of an Idea*, Harvard University Press, 1936. The name "Principle of Plenitude" seems to be a creation of Lovejoy's (*op. cit.*, p. 52.)

that a necessarily true generic proposition could not possibly have false instantiations—whereas an accidentally true one *could* have, although in
fact it has *not*.

It may be of some interest to note here Kant's attitude to the question of
the mutual relation of necessity and universality. In the Introduction to
the second edition of *Kritik der reinen Vernunft* Kant says that necessity
and strict universality are inseparably allied.[7] Kant, however, distinguished between universality which is "strict" (*streng*) and universality
which is merely "hypothetical" (*angenommen*). The second he also calls
"comparative" or "empirical". His distinction may be said to correspond
· to the one between necessary and accidental universality. Strict universality he also calls "true" (*wahr*) universality. It is therefore not clear
whether Kant would have accepted the idea of *accidental universal truth*.
He, moreover, says that universality which is merely hypothetical, really
means (*eigentlich heissen muss*) only that we have not so far met with any
exception to this or that general rule.[8]

III

Let us assume, for the sake of argument, that the only "manner" in which
a generic proposition can be universally *true* in its instantiations is by being
necessary. Must we then accept the Principle of Plenitude according to
which everything which is possible will also some time come true? The
answer is No.

Here truth-logic is of help or, more specifically, the possibility of
distinguishing between non-truth and falsehood.

Assume that instead of the equation $Np = \wedge p$ we write $Np = T \wedge p$. On
the received view of the relation between the modalities, we then also have
$\sim Np = M \sim p$. But by virtue of the above equation $M \sim p$ equals $\sim T \wedge p$.
In truth-logic $\sim T \wedge p$ equals the disjunction $T \sim \wedge p \vee \sim T \wedge p \& \sim T \sim \wedge p$.
On the received view of the relation between the quantifiers, $T \sim \wedge p$ can
also be written $T \vee \sim p$ which says that it is true that some time $\sim p$. $\sim T \wedge p$
$\& \sim T \sim \wedge p$ again says that the proposition that the generic proposition
is universal lacks truth-value, is neither true nor false.

Substituting "$\sim p$" for "p", cancelling double negation, and shifting

---

[7] "Nothwendigkeit und strenge Allgemeinheit ... gehören auch unzertrennlich zu
einander". *Kritik der reinen Vernunft*, p. 29. References are to the standard edition by the
Preussische Akademie der Wissenschaften, Vol. II.

[8] "so viel wir bisher wahrgenommen haben, findet sich von dieser oder jener Regel keine
Ausnahme". *Loc. cit.*

throughout to the existential quantifier, we also have the equality $Mp = T\lor p \lor \sim T \sim \lor p \,\&\, \sim T\lor p$. It says that a generic proposition is possible if, and only if, it either has some true instantiations *or* the proposition that it has a true instantiation is itself neither true nor false. (It is presupposed that the instantiations themselves are either true or false; cf. above p. 104).

It is thus possible to accept the idea that universal truth (of generic propositions) equals necessity and yet reject the Principle of Plenitude in the form that if a generic proposition is possible it has at least one true instantiation.

IV

Assume that neither the proposition that p nor its contradictory that $\sim p$ is necessary. The (generic) proposition in question is then contingent. Consider now the proposition that this contingent generic proposition is universal. This proposition I shall call a *synthetic universal generalization*.

It should be noted, in passing, that the proposition said to be universal is *generic*. $\land p$ says that the generic proposition that p is universal, i.e. all individual propositions instantiating it are true. But the proposition that a generic proposition is universal is itself an individual, true or false, proposition. *This* proposition I call a *universal generalization*.

It follows from what has been said above that a synthetic universal generalization either is *false* or lacks truth-value. That it is false means that there exists a false instantiation of the generic proposition, i.e. an instance which falsifies the generalization.

According to a traditional view, so-called Laws of Nature are synthetic generalizations ("from experience"). If this is combined with what has been said here about the necessary character of universal truth it follows that laws of nature either are false or lack truth-value. Or to put the same point a little differently: laws of nature are either synthetic generalizations and then possibly false *or* they are necessary truths.

The fact that synthetic (genuine) generalizations are not verifiable used to worry the early logical positivists and related philosophers. Their concern had its root in a peculiar view of *meaning and verifiability*. Propositions which are not verifiable were therefore often labelled by those thinkers as "meaningless", and excluded from "meaningful" discourse.

It was easy for the positivists to adopt this attitude to "metaphysical" propositions—it fitted their programme of fighting metaphysics. It was different with laws of nature. The positivists did not, on the whole, adopt the view that they are necessary truths (see however below pp. 137f), but regarded them as synthetic. As such they could not easily be labelled "meaningless". But there was an alternative possibility, *viz.* that of denying to laws (general hypotheses) the status of propositions. Instead of calling them propositions one sometimes called them "propositional schemas" (*Satzschema*) from which (sentences expressing) genuine propositions could be constructed through instantiation of the generalized generic proposition.[9]

---

[9] M. Schlick, "Die Kausalität in der Gegenwärtigen Physik" in *Gesammelte Aufsätze*, Gerodel, Wien 1938, p. 57, characterized laws or universal hypotheses as prescriptions or licences for the making of assertions ("Anweisungen zur Bildung von Aussagen"). See also M. Schlick, *Philosophical Papers*, Vol. II, ed. by H. Mulder and Barbara F.B. van de Velde-Schlick, D. Reidel Publishing Company, Dordrecht, Holland, 1979, p. 188. F.P. Ramsey, *The Foundations of Mathematics and Other Logical Essays*, ed. by R.B. Braithwaite, Kegan Paul, Trench; Trubner & Co., London 1931, the essay "General Propositions and Causality". Fr. Waismann, *Logik, Sprache, Philosophie*, ed. by G.P. Baker and B.F. McGuinness, Reclam, Stuttgart, 1976, pp. 612–16. L. Wittgenstein, *Philosophische Bemerkungen—Philosophical Remarks*, Basil Blackwell, Oxford 1964/1975, p. 285: "Eine Hypothese ist ein Gesetz zur Bildung von Sätzen" ("An Hypothesis is a law for forming propositions"); also *Philosophische Grammatik—Philosophical Grammar*, Basil Blackwell, Oxford 1969/1974, p. 219.

It would be of some interest to inquire into the origins of this attitude to general propositions (hypotheses, laws of nature). Schlick says (*loc. cit.*) that he owed the idea and the term (*sc.* "Anweisung zur Bildung von Aussagen") to Wittgenstein. In Victor Kraft's book *Der Wiener Kreis, der Ursprung des Neopositivismus*, Springer-Verlag, Wien, 1950, p. 123, there is a reference to the paper by Hermann Weyl, "Die heutige Erkenntnislage in der Mathematik", Symposium I, 1925, p. 19: "Ein allgemeines Urteil ist nicht ein echtes Urteil, sondern eine Urteilsanweisung". Surprisingly, the quotation cannot be found in the reprint of the article issued by Weltkreis-Verlag, Erlangen, 1926, nor in the posthumous reissue in Weyl's *Gesammelte Abhandlungen*, Band II, by Springer-Verlag, Berlin, 1968. On p. 19 of the reprint, however, we find the following sentence: "Ein Existentialsatz—etwa 'es gibt eine gerade Zahl'—ist überhaupt kein Urteil im eigentlichen Sinne, das einen Sachverhalt behauptet; Existential-Sachverhalte sind eine leere Erfindung der Logiker" ("an existential sentence—for example 'there is an even number'—is not a judgement in the real sense at all which asserts a state of affairs; existential states of affairs are an empty invention of logicians"). This very same sentence also occurs in an earlier paper by Weyl, "Über die neue Grundlagenkrise der Mathematik", published in *Mathematische Zeitschrift*, 1921. And a few lines later (*Ges. Abh.* II, p. 157) in that paper we read "Ebensowenig ist das generelle 'Jede Zahl hat die Eigenschaft E'—z.B. 'Für jede Zahl m ist $m + 1 = 1 + m$'—ein wirkliches Urteil, sondern eine generelle *Anweisung auf Urteile*" ("Similarly, the general statement 'every number has the property E'—e.g. 'For all numbers m it holds that $m + 1 = 1 + m$'—is no real judgement but a *judgement licence*"). And later in the same paper (*Ges. Abh.* II, p. 171) Weyl says "Die allgemeinen und Existentialsätze sind keine Urteile im eigentlichen Sinne, behaupten keinen Sachverhalt, sondern sind Urteilsanweisungen bzw. Urteilsabstrakte" ("Universal and existential sentences are not genuine judgements, do not assert states of affairs, but they are judgement licences or judgement abstracts").

The idea that general propositions are not "genuine", fact-stating, propositions can thus be traced to papers by Weyl from the first half of the 1920s. These papers were almost cer-

I think that this attitude to synthetic generalizations gives expression to a valuable insight. In order to preserve it, we need not label synthetic generalizations "meaningless", nor even deny to them propositional status. Such generalizations are indeed propositions, but propositions with the logical peculiarity that the only truth-value they can assume is falsehood. They can be "made true" only through an (intellectual) "act of necessitation". The nature of such "acts" we shall later (below pp. 137ff) inspect more closely.

Beside synthetic universal generalizations there are also synthetic existential generalizations. They can be verified but not falsified "in experience". Any true instantiation of the generalized generic proposition will verify it, but no "collection" of instantiations can falsify it.

Applying to existential generalizations the reasoning, *mutatis mutandis*, which we conducted above for universal generalizations one would therefore have to say that a synthetic existential generalization is either true or void of truth-value. It can be falsified only by an act of "impossibilification".

V

Let us ask now "wherein" the modal status of a generic proposition "consists".

I said above (pp. 104f) that there is a "bridge" or "bond" between the modal status of the generic proposition and the truth-values of its instantiations. Russell's attempt to "define" modal status was "reductivist". Modality, in his view, was "secondary" in relation to quantificational and truth-functional notions. It essentially depended, moreover, upon regarding statements of necessity and of universality as mutually equivalent. It had as a consequence the acceptance of the Principle of Plenitude.

I have tried to argue that one can accept a mutual equivalence between necessity and universal truth without having to subscribe to the idea that everything possible is sometimes true. This view, moreover, is not "reductivist", an attempt to "do away" with modality. It is rather an attempt to

---

tainly known to Wittgenstein. In an earlier version of the remark number 352 in the *Investigations* Wittgenstein had written "Siehe Weyl" in brackets after the quoted sentence "'In der unendlichen Entwicklung von π ....'" *This* sentence I have not found in any of the papers mentioned, and the "quotation" could very well have been made up by Wittgenstein himself. But essentially the same matter is discussed by Weyl in both the papers. Weyl in turn was indebted to Brouwer who, as we know, also was an influence on Wittgenstein. The conception of general propositions as "Urteilsanweisungen" I have not, however, found in any of Brouwer's writings.

illuminate the notion of "universal truth" with the aid of the notion of necessity, than vice-versa. It should therefore not be intrinsically palatable to those logicians and philosophers who view modality with suspicion, but are little troubled by the conceptual obscurities of quantification.

Let "p" represent a generic proposition, for example the proposition that it is raining. "$p \lor \sim p$" might then be a candidate for being a necessary (generic) proposition.

What would it *mean* that it is necessary that, say, it is raining or not raining? Must not "necessary" mean that something is *necessarily true* or *necessarily the case*? So that the question what it means to be necessary is the question what it means to be necessarily true. We must be cautious with the answer. That it is raining is a generic proposition and "as such" void of truth-value. So is the proposition that it is not raining. If the disjuncts are neither true nor false how can their disjunction be (necessarily) *true*?

The right attitude seems to me to say that that $p \lor \sim p$ is (can be) no more true and false than that p is this. The *generic* proposition that $p \lor \sim p$ is "by itself" just as void of truth-value as the generic proposition that p.

However, if a generic proposition is necessary then every instantiation of it is, not only true, but necessarily true. And vice-versa: if every instantiation of a generic proposition is necessarily true then the generic proposition is necessary. "Necessity" as an attribute of the generic proposition has then been "explained" in the terms of "necessarily true" as an attribute of its instantiations. Is this helpful?

VI

The question now is what does it mean that the individual proposition that $p_i \lor \sim p_i$ is necessarily true? For example, that at a certain time (and in a certain place) it is raining or not raining.

But is it even *true*, it may be asked, that at *any* given time t (and place l) it is either raining or not raining then (and there)? For very limited or "microscopic" spatio-temporal locations it may not be clear what it *means* to say that it is raining or not raining then and there; the notion of rainfall simply does not apply. The location must have a certain size. Which size? Must we not answer: the location must be big enough to make the proposition that it is raining in that location univocally true or false. Only if this requirement is fulfilled is it *true* that it is raining or not raining in this location. (Cf. above p. 37.)

Moreover, the notion of rainfall is not only not applicable to "microscopic" spatio-temporal locations, it is also, at the macroscopic level, vague. If only a few drops of rain are falling at rather long intervals, is it then raining or not? Probably the best thing to say here is that it is neither raining nor not-raining. Only a "logical fanatic" would refer to the Law of Excluded Middle and say that it *must be* (necessarily is) either raining or not raining at a given place at a given time.

When it is true that it is raining it is also true, by implication, that it is raining or not raining—and similarly when it is true that it is not raining. Even if one thinks of the *implication* $p_i \rightarrow p_i \lor \sim p_i$ as necessary one could not say that it shows that the disjunction $p_i \lor \sim p_i$ is necessary. On the contrary, does not the fact that some instantiations of the generic proposition that p are neither true nor false show that the generic proposition that $p \lor \sim p$ is *not* necessary?

Perhaps our example—rainfall—was biased since it did not satisfy the schema $\land(Tp \lor T \sim p)$. In the case of some other generic proposition(s) it may appear "undeniable" that every instantiation is either true or false (= its contradictory true). But that *this* is not necessarily so for all generic propositions is shown by our example—and in a more general way by the possibility of constructing a "truth-logic" in which the Law of Bivalence is not universally valid.

In our truth-logic we proved that it is true that $p_i \lor \sim p_i$ if, and only if, it is true that p_i or false that p_i. $T(p_i \lor \sim p_i) \leftrightarrow Tp_i \lor T \sim p_i$ is a theorem of this logic, but the membra of the equivalence are not theorems.

But could we not avoid these complications if instead of looking for necessarily true instantiations of the Principle of Bivalence, $Tp_i \lor T \sim p_i$, we consider instantiations of that version of the Law of Excluded Middle which holds in our truth-logic. This says that any proposition is either true or *not* (true): $Tp \lor \sim Tp$ (see above, p. 33). So, even if it is not always necessarily true that it is raining or not raining, since in some instances it is neither raining nor not-raining, it is nevertheless always necessary that it is either true that it is raining or is not true that it is raining.

But this manoeuvre will not help. It is true that in our truth-logic it is true that any (individual) proposition is either true or not, and not true that every (individual) proposition is either true or false. But must it be so *necessarily*? Must a truth-logic be so constructed that $Tp \lor \sim Tp$ is a theorem in it? Is there of necessity only *one* "true" truth-logic?

Our system TL was built with the specific purpose in mind to "cater" for the existence of propositions which are neither true nor false. It was relatively easy to suggest examples. One type of example was provided by cases of vagueness. "Between" the states of raining and of not-raining there fall unclear cases of which it is not (univocally) true to say that it is raining nor to say that it is not raining. But there are also clear cases. Is it, however, always clear whether a case is a clear case, or not? "Between" the clear and the unclear cases there may be cases of which we might be in doubt as how to classify them. Someone may without hesitation say: "True: it is still raining, I feel drops falling on my bare head." Another may answer: "So do I, but the drops are too few and far apart to constitute rainfall; rainfall has not ceased completely, but it is also not true that it is still raining." After a while, when drops become even rarer, they both agree that it would *not* be true to say that it is raining.

This imagined conversation is designed to show that, just as one can drive "a wedge of indeterminacy" between "clear" states that p and that not p for which that Tp and that $T \sim p$ respectively hold good, one can also drive a similar wedge between clear cases when Tp and when not Tp. Thus one is admitting, in addition to a possibility of $\sim Tp \,\&\, \sim T \sim p$ also a possibility $\sim TTp \,\&\, \sim T \sim Tp$. The second corresponds to an even finer "grading" or "shading" of states in the world. *Our* TL cannot cater for this finer structuring, since in it the formula $\sim TTp \,\&\, \sim T \sim Tp$ is refutable, "logically false". But it is perfectly possible to construct a truth-logic in which this is not so, i.e. in which the Law of Excluded Middle does not hold good *even* in the very weak form which says that any given (individual) proposition is either true or not (true).

What is the moral taught by this for necessity? It is obvious that whenever one has a reason for doubting or denying that all instantiations of a given generic proposition are (even) *true* one cannot pronounce the generic proposition itself *necessary*. But even if there were no such doubts, say about the universal validity of the "Law of Excluded Middle", it does not seem feasible to try to explain the necessity of the generic proposition by referring to the necessary truth of its instances. The question of truth of an instantiation can be settled independently of the question of its necessity. Must not the source of necessity, if there is any necessity at all, reside in the generic proposition as its *"Urbild"* or standard?

It is clear that the necessity of a generic proposition and the necessary truth of its instantiations are what would be called in German *Wechselbegriffe*. If the generic proposition is necessary its instantiations are necessarily true and vice-versa. But to try to elucidate the first necessity by means of the second seems like exploring a blind alley. We must therefore turn round and try a different direction.

VII

Consider again the proposition that it is raining or not raining. We could adopt to it the following attitude: we use it for dividing the states of weather prevailing in certain spatio-temporal areas into two mutually exclusive and jointly exhaustive classes: rain and not-rain. If the spatio-temporal areas are neither too big nor too small, roughly answering to what we mean when, speaking about the weather, we call "here" and "now", this principle of classification would be applicable without difficulty to nearly all cases. Perhaps there are a few situations when we could not easily say whether it is raining or not raining but would have to *decide* in favour of the one or the other. We then *insist* upon the mutually exclusive and jointly exhaustive character of the two alternatives.

I maintain that it is in this, or a similar, attitude that the *logical necessity* of the generic proposition that it is raining or not raining "consists". Or rather: this attitude "confers" necessity on the proposition. We insist *"a priori"* on its applicability for the purpose of separating states of the weather into two mutually exclusive and jointly exhaustive classes, thus also making all its individual instantiations "necessarily true".

Our attitude may change. Assume that there are very many cases when we cannot easily tell whether it is raining or not but are "forced" to make a decision. We may then abandon our insistence on the mutually exclusive and jointly exhaustive nature of the two alternatives and reserve room for a third category or state of weather when it is neither raining nor not raining. Then the proposition that it is either raining or not raining is no longer necessary, i.e. it is no longer *treated* as such.

We can "logicize" the changed attitude, for example by saying that the proposition that it is raining is either true or false or lacks truth-value. Then we could deal with it in a logic like our TL. But we could also say that we distinguish between a weaker and stronger way of denying the proposition that it is raining, or between two types of negation: not raining and not-raining. Then we may treat "it is raining or not raining" as necessary, but not "it is raining or not-raining".

We regard or treat some generic propositions as necessary as long as this attitude to them gives us a useful instrument for describing reality. Applicability, not truth, is what sanctions talk of necessity here. Some such generic propositions, for example those which are disjunctions of another (generic) proposition and its negation, can be taken to exemplify propositional (sentential) schemas, such as $p \lor \sim p$, and the schemas systematized in a logical calculus, e.g. "classical" PL or our TL. Other necessary generic propositions have a more *ad hoc* character. They do not belong in a system of "laws of logic". We shall later have to say something about them too (below, pp. 137ff).

No system of logic can establish the necessity of its own principles (axioms, theorems). Nothing is necessary "by virtue of the laws of logic" alone. Necessity stems from an attitude we take to some propositions or, which is the same, from a way of applying and using some sentences. And the "laws" of a logic exemplify propositions to which such an attitude is usually, or for some purposes, taken.

Someone may wish to label my view of logical necessity—and of the modal status generally of generic propositions—"conventionalist", "linguistic" or even "subjectivist". Each label would have some justification—but each one would also be misleading.

Wittgenstein criticized[10] the idea of "the hardness of the logical must" and the prejudice of the "crystalline purity of logic". He was fighting, I think, against the same tendency to *mystify necessity* which I try to avoid myself by saying that necessity is conferred on propositions by certain attitudes we take to them and ways in which we treat them—and not by a "preformed" logical structure of the world itself.

To view or to *treat* a generic proposition as *necessary*, one could say, is to *insist on the truth* of its instantiations. It is to take an *a priori attitude* to a whole class of individual propositions; to exempt them from verification ("through experience") and yet pronounce them true. When this attitude is taken we say of the individual propositions that they are "necessarily true".

Similarly, to treat a generic proposition as *impossible* is to insist "*a priori*" on the falsity of (all) its instantiations. It is to exclude it from truth prior to falsification, one could also say.

In the absence of a "necessitating" or "impossibilifying" *a priori* attitude to a generic proposition we regard it as *contingent*, i.e. we are prepared to accept a verifying or a falsifying verdict on its truth-value in each individual instance. Its instantiations, we say, are contingently true or contingently false "as the case may be". We may conjecture that a false instantiation will never be found. This is to make what we have called earlier (p. 108) a synthetic generalization to the effect that the generic proposition is universal. The generalization may be falsified but cannot be verified. Sometimes, however, we pronounce such a generalization true "*a priori*" thus removing it from possible falsification and thereby deciding to treat the corresponding generic proposition as necessary. There may be good reasons for this change of attitude to its modal status (cf. later pp. 137ff).

VIII

The modalities which I have been discussing in this essay I propose to call *logical*. The necessity (possibility, contingency) under consideration has been *logical* necessity (possibility, etc.).

---

[10] *PU* I, 107–8, 437.

In the view which I have taken, the modal status of a generic proposition is primary in relation to the modal status of its instantiations. By virtue of the generic proposition being logically necessary its instantiations may be pronounced logically necessary too; and similarly for the other modal attributes.

The modal status of a generic proposition, moreover, is "reflected" in the relation of its instantiations to truth. All instantiations of a necessary generic proposition are true, and all instantiations of an impossible generic proposition are false. They are this "necessarily", that is: (because) we insist upon their truth and falsehood respectively—regardless of "the testimony of experience".

A true instantiation of a generic proposition is also a logically possible proposition. That is: the generic proposition is possible and thereby also each one of its instantiations, whether true or false. It is not, however, the *truth* of the instantiation which "shows" or "proves" that the generic proposition is (logically) *possible*. Logical possibility is a presupposition of truth. "In order to be true it has to be possible" is the correct logical order, and not "it is possible, since it is true".[11] But then it should again be remembered that what constitutes the logical possibility of the generic proposition is an attitude we take to the relation of its instantiations to truth.

I have here discussed the logical modalities only in relation to generic propositions (propositional functions) and their instantiations as partaking in the modal status of the propositions which they instantiate. In doing this I have not wished to deny or exclude that there are individual propositions which are logically necessary, possible, etc. "in their own right" so to say and not *qua* instantiations of some generic proposition. Simple arithmetic truths, such as for instance that $7 + 5 = 12$, may serve as examples. How to conceive of their modal status is a problem which, however, falls outside the scope of the present inquiry.

---

[11] Cf. Wittgenstein's criticism of Russell's view of modality in the *Tractatus*.

Natural Modality

I

The attitudes which are reflected in the modal status of generic propositions are not "absolute" in the sense that they were "eternal and immutable". They are flexible and susceptible to change (see below, p. 139 and above, p. 114). But attributions of logical modality are in the following sense *atemporal*: if we take the view that a generic proposition is logically necessary (possible, contingent, impossible) we commit ourselves to the view that the same modal status pertains to all its instantiations, regardless of when and where they materialize. If our attitude changes, this change affects also all instantiations which happened to have materialized when our previous attitude prevailed. One could call the change in attitude a change in *conception* of the generic proposition and also speak, though with caution, of two different generic propositions.

There is another type of attribution of modal status which is specifically *temporal*. Something is thought to be necessary, possible, etc. at a certain moment or sometimes or (even) always. And the very same thing which is thought to be possible at one time may be deemed impossible at another time.

The type of modal status which I have in mind I shall call *natural* or *physical* or *causal*. (I shall here treat the three terms as synonyms.)

The "things" to which this kind of modal status is attributed are propositions. Generic or individual? it may be asked. The answer is that both types of proposition are capable of such modal status. But, unlike what was the case with the logical modalities, one cannot from the physical modal status of the generic proposition conclude the modal status of its instantiations, nor vice-versa.

When speaking in the following of individual propositions, I always mean instantiations in time of some generic proposition—for example of the proposition that p at t (p_t) as an instantiation of the generic proposition that p, say the proposition that it is raining.

II

We consider first individual propositions. At time t' the proposition that p at t is deemed necessary or possible, etc. This can be written, using our previous symbolism, as follows: $N_{t'}p_t$, $M_{t'}p_t$, etc.

Three possibilities can now be distinguished: t' is either earlier than, simultaneous with, or later than t. In the first and third case I shall call the modality *diachronic*, in the second case *synchronic*.

Of the diachronic modal attributions one can distinguish two types: *prospective*, corresponding to the first of the three cases above, and *retrospective*, corresponding to the third case.

With the prospective case we have already dealt, from a formal logical point of view, in the essay "Diachronic and Synchronic Modality". We shall not say anything more here about the formal logical aspects.

We have also dealt with a special case of retrospective diachronic modality, *viz.* the Diodorean idea that "what is true and past is necessary" (see above, pp. 75f). I interpreted it as meaning that if it is true that p at t then at any time t' later than t it is necessary that p at t. If we regard the present as a limiting point of the past, the Aristotelian thesis that "what is is necessary when it is" follows as a corollary.

One can raise the following question about the Diodorean–Aristotelian thesis: is the necessity involved "natural" or "logical"? From the way in which I have here defined attributions of natural modality it would follow that the necessity of the past and present is natural necessity. This, I think, is in order, because the "point" of the thesis, as I understand it, is that it captures a feature of the causal relation, *viz.* that causal efficacy is "forward-looking" (see above, p. 81). One can argue that this is a logical (conceptual) point about causality and that therefore the truth of the *thesis*, if accepted as true at all, is *logical* and thus necessary. One can also argue that it is a factual (empirical) feature about the causal relation. To me the first way of arguing seems better. Accepting it—and received truths of modal logic—one could then say that it is *logically* necessary that it is necessary at t' that p at t if it is true that p at t and t' is later than t. But this does not allow the conclusion that therefore it is *logically* necessary at t' that p at t.

Nothing further will be said here about retrospective diachronic modality.

III

Before turning to a closer study of prospective diachronic modalities we make a brief detour to temporalized attributions of modality to *generic* propositions.

According to the scholarly tradition, Diodorus Cronus taught that the possible either is or will (some time) be true, and the necessary, accordingly, is and will (always) be true.

It is natural, even if not compelling, to understand such "Diodorean" attributions as temporalized. Something is possible *now* if it is either true now or will be true at some time in the future; something was possible *ten years ago* if it was either true then or came true or will come true later. It follows that what was possible ten years ago need not be possible any longer; it once came true, let us assume, five years ago but neither was nor will ever be repeated.

"That which" comes or does not come true is a generic proposition, call it "*p*". The Diodorean definition of possibility can thus be expressed in symbols as follows: $M_t p =_{df} (Et')(t \leqslant t' \& p_{t'})$, and the definition of necessity: $N_t p =_{df} (t')(t \leqslant t' \rightarrow p_{t'})$.

Diodorean modalities must be understood to be "natural" and not "logical". This is best seen from the fact that the Diodorean definitions allow for *changes* in modal status (of one and the same generic proposition). Something which was possible is perhaps no longer possible; and something which was not necessary before is necessary now. Such changes seem fully compatible with common notions about what is *physically* (naturally) possible or necessary. But it would be highly unnatural to say of a generic proposition which had one true instantiation but never another one that it lost its "logical possibility" of coming true after that instantiation.

The Diodorean definitions are obviously intended to be valid for all values of the time variable *t*. This means that they entail (subscribe to) the Principle of Plenitude (cf. above, p. 106).

As far as attribution of modal status to generic propositions is concerned, the Diodorean definitions are *reductivist*. They define the modal status of such propositions in the terms of truth and quantification.

It is of some interest to compare Diodorus's view with another reductivist theory of modality, *viz.* the one which Russell professed in several of his writings. Russell's view may be characterized as a "generalization" or, better, "omnitemporalization" of Diodorus's. In Russell's view, in symbolic terms: $Mp =_{df} (Et)p_t$ and $Np =_{df} (t)p_t$ (see above pp. 105f).

The main difference between the two views is that Russell's excludes change in modal status. "Once possible, always possible", one could say. This is why no time-index is needed for the modal operator; and this is why it is not unnatural to regard *his* view as pertaining (also) to those modalities which we think of as "logical" as distinct from "natural" or "physical".

IV

Some philosophers, particularly such of a "positivist" turn of mind, might find the Diodorean, and maybe even the Russellian, view acceptable as an account of the *natural* modalities. One would then think that the only "proof" there can be that something is physically possible is that this thing comes true. One may regard it as a corollary to this view that something is physically possible *at a certain time* if, and only if, it is true at that time. Aristotle's *dictum* that that which is is necessary when it is would then be (trivially) true for physical necessity.

It seems to me obvious, however, that many more interesting things can be said about the natural modalities. This is so even if one will, eventually, arrive at the view that the logical and the natural modalities are "essentially" the same kind of modality (see later, p. 137).

Diodorus can be said to have taken a "prospectivist" view of the modal notions. Whether something is, in his view, possible or necessary depends upon what is or will happen with regard to it. A "retrospectivist" view may seem more natural, at least to us moderns. This means to let the modal status of a proposition depend upon what is the case at the time of its truth or, perhaps, upon things which were the case before it came true and, so to say, "prepared the ground" for the possibility or necessity of the proposition in question.

So let our question be: what do we mean when we say that, at a certain time, it is necessary or possible that something is at that same time or will be at a later time? What, in other words, is the meaning of our symbolic expressions $N_{t'}p_t$ and $M_{t'}p_t$, when $t' \leqslant t$?

There is an answer ready at hand: that it is physically necessary at t' that p at t means that it is a "law of nature" that, under the then, i.e. from t' to t, prevailing circumstances, we shall call them "C", it has to be that p at t. And that this same thing is physically possible at t' means that it is not a "law of nature" that under those circumstances it has to be that not-p at t. (Instead of the phrase "it is a 'law of nature' that", I could also have said "there is a 'law of nature' (to the effect) that".)

V

Few people would perhaps disagree with this suggested "elucidation" but many would presumably say that it is completely unilluminating. And some would perhaps add that, not only does it not illuminate, it obscures the issue. It tries to explain natural modality with reference to "laws of nature". But what are they? Can we explain this without making reference to natural modality?

I think that the last question need not constitute a worry. But the penultimate one must be answered. Before embarking on a discussion of it, let us for the time being focus attention on the suggested elucidations of the expressions $N_{t'}p_t$ and $M_{t'}p_t$.

Of the circumstances C we already said that their "prevailing" should be understood to cover the time-interval from t' to t, inclusive. The "prevailing" does not (necessarily) exclude changes among the circumstances; changes, that is, which are irrelevant to the "identity" of C.

The elucidations, as seen, make necessity the basic or primary idea. Natural possibility is the absence of impossibility, i.e. of a necessity to the contrary; so further elucidations will have to focus on the idea of natural *necessity*.

We distinguished previously (p. 100) two forms of necessity, strong and weak. That p at t was said to be in the strong sense (synchronically) necessary if, and only if, it was (diachronically) antecedently necessary from *always* before ("from the dawn of creation")—and in the weak sense if, and only if, it was this from *some time t'* before. Strong necessity is, trivially, also weak. Non-trivially, necessity is weak when it is *not* also strong, i.e. when something which from some time t' on will necessarily be at a certain time t was not necessary before t', i.e. when a *change in modal status* has taken place (at t'). Change here means that something which was possible becomes impossible, or which was possible becomes necessary. For reasons, given before (pp. 98f), we regard changes in the other direction as "logically excluded": the physically impossible cannot become physically possible. This last must not be misunderstood: an instantiation of a certain generic proposition at a given time may be impossible, but later instantiations of the very same generic proposition may perfectly well be possible and sometimes perhaps even necessary.

A change in modal status of a generic proposition can also be termed a case of *necessitation* (of the individual proposition which is necessary after the change).

In order to cut out trivialities we shall throughout the following discussion assume that the generic propositions, to the instantiations of which (natural) modal status is attributed, are *logically contingent*.

VI

The logical modalities as discussed by us here applied primarily to generic propositions and in a secondary sense to their instantiations. The natural or physical modalities as defined by us apply primarily to individual propositions. Can they be applied to generic propositions (except in the "prospectivist" sense defined by Diodorus)?

Some caution is needed when answering this question.

One might suggest the following definitions: a generic proposition is necessary when all its instantiations are antecedently necessary, and contingent when some instantiations of it but also some of its contradictory are antecedently possible. But if this is the suggestion one must also settle the following question: should antecedent necessity here be understood in the strong or in the weak sense (and correspondingly for possibility)?

If understood in the weak sense, some instantiations of the contradictory of a necessary generic proposition may be antecedently possible. Since what is antecedently necessary is also antecedently possible, it would then follow that the same generic proposition may be both physically necessary and physically contingent. This may be thought awkward. In order to secure that modal status belongs univocally to generic propositions one would have to say that a generic proposition is necessary only if all its instantiations are in the *strong* sense antecedently necessary. (And similarly for generic impossibility.)

Accepting this precisation of the initial suggestion one would then have to notice the following: instantiations of a contingent generic proposition may themselves be necessary or impossible, even in the strong sense of "necessary" and "impossible". Moreover, this may be the case with *all* its instantiations! Example: it is sometimes raining, sometimes not raining. This is enough to show that the generic proposition that it is raining is naturally or physically or causally contingent. ("*Ab esse ad posse valet consequentia.*") But every single instance of rainfall may nevertheless be a natural necessity and similarly, though this would be an even more demanding case, every single instance when it is not raining.

As seen from this example, the (natural) modal status of a generic proposition may be different from the modal status of some, or even all, its instantiations. A convinced determinist would say that all instantiations of contingent generic propositions are, in fact, either necessary or impossible.

A generic proposition which is a natural necessity is also universal; but the converse does not hold. Some of the instances of a universal proposition may be necessary, either in the strong or the weak sense, but others may be contingent, i.e. their contradictories in the strong sense antecedently possible.

A (physically) necessary individual proposition which instantiates a (physically) contingent generic proposition can be called a *contingent necessity*. This is useful terminology which we shall here employ (see also above, pp. 55 and 101.)

When speaking of an individual proposition it is sometimes convenient to refer to the modal status of the generic proposition which it instantiates as its (i.e. the individual proposition's) modal status "at the generic level", contrasting it with its modal status "at the individual level".

VII

We must inspect more closely the notion of antecedent necessity. We shall first consider its weak form only, and the ideas related to it of change in modal status and of necessitation. Our question will be: how can something which was not necessary before, be so from a certain time on?

We return to the example which we gave (above, p. 99) of a person who is killed in an explosion at *t* and of whom we would say that from time *t'* on he was "doomed", and could not possibly have escaped the fatal end. What could be our grounds for saying this?

Let us, for the sake of simplicity, assume that the explosion, too, occurred at *t*. The death of the unhappy person was, more or less, "instant". What does it mean to say that his death was *caused* by the explosion? Calling the explosion "cause" is a rather complex statement. A stuff exploded and in doing so generated a very strong blast in combination, maybe, with terrific heat and the bursting of a shell and whirling about of splinters. One can trace these "manifestations" of the explosion back to generating factors and "identify" the explosion itself with some of them, perhaps at a "microscopic" level. The manifestations would then be the effect of the explosion as their cause. But one can also say that the manifestations constitute the explosion, or aspects of it. In either case these manifestations then "hit" the victim; his body was exposed to them and could not sustain their effect(s) on it; so he died. If we say that his death then was necessary we mean, roughly, that under similar circumstances (of an explosion) no human body (or perhaps no human body of a similar, say frail, constitution) within a certain radius from the centre of an explosion could stay alive. In saying this we enunciate, in a rough and primitive way, a "law of nature" to the effect that whenever there is an explosion thus strong and a(n unprotected) human being thus near it the outcome will be fatal. This element of generality or universality seems essential to the statement that the person's death was, under the circumstances, inevitable, necessary. Scientists may be able to give to the assumed law-connection(s) here a much more precise formulation, and thus partly explain to us *why* a human body cannot sustain an explosion of this strength at that distance. But this is not essential to our view of the person's death as a "necessity" under the circumstances.

So far nothing has been said about "antecedent necessity". The explosion necessitated the person's death at *t* but why say that he was "doomed" from *t'* on?

By the "fatal area" we shall understand the area, surrounding the centre of the explosion, within which a human body cannot withstand the effects of the explosion. The victim is supposed to have been at time t' within this area and could not have transported himself beyond its boundaries in the time-interval from t' to t. What does "could not" mean here? Perhaps it means "however fast he had run away from the place". But what if he had had a car or motorbike at his disposal? We assume that he had none. Nor was there a helicopter to take him away. But *could* there not have been one? Is this not at least *logically* possible? Perhaps we can imagine this—but the *fact* is that there was no such means of rescue then. "Under the circumstances" he was doomed to die in the explosion.

The person might for some time already have been at the place where he was at t'. But before t' he *could* have rescued himself, e.g. by running away. It was a contingent fact that at t' he was where he happened to be. It is also a contingent fact that the explosion took place at t. There might have been something which necessitated the explosion, some antecedent cause of it. Perhaps a time-bomb had been placed there. But this is irrelevant to the statement that the death of the person in question was antecedently necessary. It is relevant that the explosion took place at t—but whether this was an absolute contingency or something which was in its turn necessitated by something else is not relevant.

The *cause* of the person's death was the explosion. *It* took place at t and "necessitated" the death—(more or less) "instantaneously" we assume. (Whether a cause can be strictly simultaneous with its effect is a problem to which we shall return; see below, pp. 127f. (At t' nothing of the sort happened. Even if the person had not already for some time been where he was at t', but just then arrived at that place, neither the state of his being there nor the event of his arriving could rightly be said to have *caused* his death. Only if something which happened at t' had necessitated ("released") the explosion at t could this (by transitivity) be said to have caused his death. (And it might of course be true that the person's arrival at that place actually caused the explosion. But it need not be true.)

The analysis of this example shows that something which happens at time t can be antecedently necessary from a certain earlier time t' on (but not before then) without anything being the case or happening at t' which would be a cause, necessitating the event at t.

Although it is right to say that at t' it became antecedently necessary that the person should die at t, it is also right to say that this became so *only in retrospect*, i.e. by virtue of the fact that something happened later (the explosion) which, viewing things from t', was a contingency. An explosion at a certain time does not kill any man unless the circumstances are such that there *is* a man then within the "fatal area" of the explosion. The effect (death) of the cause (explosion) may be necessary "under the circumstances" but contingent upon the prevailing of those circumstances. And the circumstances may be such that no change in them after a certain time is (physically) possible which would have prevented the effect once the cause was there.

VIII

In order to pronounce something, *e*, which happens at *t* antecedently necessary from *t'* on, it is required that there is something, *c*, which causes or necessitates *e* to take place at *t*. The necessitating "bond" between *c* and *e* has the character of a "law of nature" which is such that whenever *c* then also *e* under the circumstances *C* which prevail over the interval from *t'* to *t*. I shall say that the circumstances constitute a "contingency clause" and that the law involves a universal regularity under a contingency clause.

In the example which we discussed in the preceding section, it was assumed that *c* (the explosion) was simultaneous with *e* (the death of the person). But this need not be so; perhaps it cannot even be (exactly) so. The explosion might also have occurred earlier, at some time *t″* between *t'* and *t*.

Assume now that this was, in fact, the case. Then one could "divide" the time during which the death of the person at *t* was antecedently necessary into two "periods" or "phases". The first is from *t'* to *t″* when the death of the person was a necessity because something occurred at *t″* (the explosion) which necessitated his death at *t* and which is such that he could not have escaped its effect by anything that he might have done or which might have happened to him after *t'*. The second phase was from *t″* to *t* when the death of the person was necessary because there was the explosion and the person happened to be in the "fatal area". But when did this "become" necessary? At the time of the explosion *t″*? Or at the time of his death *t*?

Saying that the explosion caused the death, not instantly, at *t″*, but after some time, at *t*, is to make implicit reference to a regularity under a contingency clause. Perhaps the person hit by the explosion would not have died had he been taken to hospital in time *or* had he been subject to such and such treatment which was not available in the hospital where he was taken (but perhaps would have been available in another one), *or* ...
But nothing of this which might have prevented the explosion from having its fatal effect happened or was the case. If one is confident that none of these life-saving things could happen in the interval from *t″* to *t* (no rescue could be there earlier, the distance to a better-equipped hospital is far too great, etc.), one would say "right away", i.e. at *t″*, that he is

doomed to die. But as long as some such possibilities are thought to be open we would not say this. When he dies the door of possibilities is mercilessly closed—under the circumstances as they were (throughout the interval from t'' to t) it is *now* (at t) clear that his death was antecedently necessary from t''. (Provided we are prepared to say that under those circumstances an explosion will regularly result in death, if not instantly, after some time.)

As we see from this discussion, the antecedent necessity from a certain time of something that takes place at a later time is dependent on contingencies which might arise in the meantime and which must be excluded before the attribution of antecedent necessity can take place. If they are excluded *before* that later time this can only be because we think of them as physical impossibilities. Only at that later time itself are they *logically* excluded, *viz.* excluded by virtue of the "logical fact" that the past cannot be changed. If by the exclusion of contingencies we mean exclusion in this strong sense, then any attribution of antecedent necessity $N_{t'}p_t$ is *retrospective* in the sense that it only becomes definite *at* t, i.e. when that to which it is attributed is (already) a fact.

IX

That a proposition which is or comes true at t is in the *weak* sense contingently necessary (already) at t' entails that at some time before t' the proposition that not-p at t was antecedently possible. This, we have said, is "physical possibility". Since the truth of that p at t warrants (for reasons of logic) that the proposition that p at t was always antecedently possible, it follows that the proposition that p at t was physically *contingent* some time before t' although it subsequently became physically *necessary*. That this change in its modal status should occur presupposes normally that something else came true which necessitated that p at t. This necessitating factor, however, need not have been there at t'. It may also have occurred later, although—"retrospective causation" being excluded—not later than t. If its occurrence was itself a contingency, not necessitated by anything at t' or earlier, then the attribution of antecedent necessity to the proposition that p_t at t' was an attribution so to say "in retrospect". How this can happen was, I think, shown by the analysis of the example of the man who died in the explosion. But the analysis also showed that this "retrospective conferring of antecedent necessity" is subject to what we called a *contingency clause* saying that nothing will happen after t' which prevents the cause of that p at t from having this effect (*viz.* that p at t). And our analysis of the necessitating relation which an antecedent cause has to this same effect is subject to an analogous contingency clause concerning the time from when the cause occurs to the time of the effect.

The preventive interferences which the contingency clauses exclude are themselves physical possibilities at the generic level. Some of them may contingently not materialize before *t*, but others may be physical impossibilities (their negations necessities) by virtue of something which took place already before *t'*. (It should be remembered that that which is physically possible at the generic level can *also* be physically impossible at the level of individuation; cf. above, p. 122.) And some of these impossibilities may be known or regarded as "practical certainties" not to be taken into account when pronouncing it antecedently necessary that *p* at *t*. It is, however, only at *t* that it can be *established* that no preventive interference actually occurred and also that the antecedent necessity of that *p* at *t* was there from some time *t'* in what is then already the past. One could therefore say, with an air of paradox, that only at *t* does it "become" necessary from *t'* on that *p* at *t*.

One could also say that weak antecedent necessity is "doubly contingent". It is contingent in the sense that the proposition which is necessary from a certain time on was contingent in the perspective which prevailed before that time. And it is contingent in the sense that no preventive interference which was physically possible took place after the time from which the proposition is deemed antecedently necessary.

X

A discussion of weak necessity involving a change in the modal status of an individual proposition thus points in the direction of an identification of such change with necessitation of something by something else in virtue of a "law of nature".

When necessity is antecedent, the necessitating factor normally occurs before that which it necessitates. But is (genuine) weak necessity always and necessarily *antecedent*, i.e. does the synchronic weak necessity of the proposition that *p* at *t* require that this proposition was necessary already before *t*, at least for some short time, due to the appearance of a necessitating factor? Or can the necessitating factor (the cause) be *simultaneous* with the thing it necessitates (the effect)?

It is sometimes thought that a time-gap is needed here in order to make it possible to distinguish the two factors as cause and effect respectively. If they were absolutely simultaneous, would not then the effect also be cause, and the cause effect? But the causal relation surely must be asymmetrical, we think.

The separation of cause and effect when the two are simultaneous is certainly problematic. A solution to the problem may be sought, however, along the following lines:

The separation of cause and effect presupposes that three conditions are satisfied. First, that, under some different circumstances from those when they occur together, the two events can and will happen *independently*, i.e. the cause without yielding that effect and the effect without having that cause. Secondly, that the occurrence of the cause at *t*, and generally on all occasions when it produces the effect under consideration, can in its turn be traced back to something antecedent, an event or a process, which is held causally responsible for its occurrence then. And thirdly, that this second condition is not fulfilled, at *t*, for the effect, i.e. we cannot connect *it* with an independent antecedent causal factor.

Consider again our explosion example. Explosions may take place without any casualties—and most people do not die as victims of an explosion. Thus the cause-event and the effect-event are clearly separable at the *generic* level. The explosion presumably had an antecedent cause, e.g. someone struck a match and ignited something which then, some moments later, released the explosion. The person's death we cannot, let us assume, trace back to anything antecedent. It is, of course, possible that he died of a stroke which would have occurred even if there had been no explosion. Then the effect, his death, would have been overdetermined. It is, moreover, possible (perhaps) that the explosion happened without any antecedent cause. Even then, however, we would think that *it* caused the death of the person—and not the other way round, because we know from other instances that explosions may cause death. We can think of extraordinary circumstances under which the death of a person may actually release an explosion; but the circumstances, we assume, were not in this way extraordinary in the case under discussion.

To relate two simultaneous occurrences as cause and effect relative to each other thus requires that normally one of them has a "causal history", emerges from the past as the effect of some antecedent cause. The word "normally" is added in order to provide for the possibility that the cause-event itself occurs causelessly, spontaneously *in this case*—a possibility which some may doubt but which I think should be conceded in order to avoid "deterministic dogmatism". But one can allow this possibility only if one assumes familiarity at the *generic* level with causal antecedents of the supposed cause in the individual case under discussion. So one can safely conclude that admitting simultaneous causation presupposes familiarity with antecedent causation. Synchronic necessitation, one could therefore say, is *secondary* to diachronic.

In spite of these concessions in favour of the possibility of simultaneous causation, some doubts may remain. One can readily agree that cause and effect may be "practically simultaneous", and may occur on the same occasion if the occasion is allowed a certain duration and is not limited to just a "point" in time. With this kind of "simultaneity" in causal relationships we are all familiar. The "instantaneous" death of a person in an explosion is presumably as good an example as any. But the question may be raised whether, after all, causation can be "absolutely" or *strictly* simultaneous.

It is obvious that the explosion example is *not* one of "absolute" simultaneity. The heat, pressure, splinters, and what not generated by the explosion had to hit and affect the person's body with a certain force in order to kill him. Surely these processes, "linking" the cause (the explosion) with the effect (the person's death) were processes of some duration, and not "instantaneous" happenings. Thus, speaking here of "simultaneous causation" presupposes, it seems, an occasion which is itself extended in time and may be subdivided into bits or phases, beginning with the explosion and ending with the death of the victim.

In another place I have discussed the causal connection between the opening and shutting of two valves which are connected by a rod or other mechanism so that they move strictly at the same time.[1] In this case there seem to be no processes "mediating" between cause and effect; but here, too, an antecedent cause of the supposedly simultaneous cause is, in the normal cases, needed.

XI

I said that, normally, when there is a change in modal status of a proposition, i.e. when a proposition, the contradictory of which was possible up to a certain time t', is necessary after that time, there is a "necessitating factor" responsible for this change. The precise nature of this factor—whether it must be that something which was not comes to be or whether it can also be that something which is does not change—we did not discuss; nor shall we discuss it now. It suffices for our purposes to stipulate that the factor in question shall consist, at least, in the fact that a certain proposition is true before t. Thus one can say, for example, that q at t' necessitated that p at t, and thereby is also responsible for the truth of that $N_{t'}p_t$.

Must there always exist such a necessitating factor? Or is it possible ("thinkable") that a proposition becomes necessary from a certain time on

---

[1] *Causality and Determinism*, pp. 63–8.

without any such necessitating cause? Can there be, speaking figuratively, "spontaneous creation" of necessity?

Be it noted in passing that if $N_{t'}p_t$ can come true without the appearance, at t', of a necessitating factor, then this would presumably also hold for $N_t p_t$, meaning that something can become necessary right at the moment when it comes true. If we think this possible we must abandon our previous elucidation of the meaning of synchronic necessity in diachronic terms. To refuse to do this *a priori* would seem dogmatic.

It is difficult to imagine anything which would tempt us to say that from t' on it was necessary that p at t, if we cannot back up this statement with some reasons, (such as, e.g., the occurrence of a necessitating cause). Must there not, at least, be something peculiar about the circumstances C which prevailed over the interval from t' to t, but not before t', warranting the necessity of the truth of that p at t? But if so, then this peculiar feature of C which was not there before t' would be a "cause" necessitating that p at t; and we should not have a case of "spontaneous creation" of necessity.

Imagine the following case:

The state that p comes to obtain with great regularity in time. Then it "instantly" vanishes again; so that, say, if it is true that p at t then it will again be true that p five minutes later, and again five minutes after that and so forth. As far as we have been able to ascertain, this regularity is quite independent of the "accompanying circumstances", such as temperature, atmospheric pressure, illumination, etc. It is simply a "Law of Nature" that such is the case with regard to the state that p.

Now at t' it comes true that p. Thereafter, we could say, is the proposition antecedently necessary that p is true at t, when t is the time five minutes after t'. But if the Law of Nature entitles us to say this it also entitles us to say that p at t was antecedently necessary already any time before t', in fact "from the dawn of creation". The modal nature of the proposition has never changed—it was always necessary. So in this imagined case too there is no "spontaneous" origination of necessity.

Are there such laws of nature—"purely temporal regularities" as they might be called? Is perhaps the regularity with which atoms of the elements disintegrate something *resembling* the example we gave? These questions may not be uninteresting in themselves; but they are irrelevant to the question we initially raised, *viz.* whether something can become antecedently necessary without the occurrence of a necessitating factor. The answer to *this* question seems to be negative: either the antecdent necessity depends on some circumstantial feature which contains a necessitating cause *or* the necessity is there from "the dawn of creation".

XII

The necessitating factor which effects a change in the modal status of a proposition may either occur contingently or be necessitated by another necessitating factor. We may have, for example, $N_{t'}p_t$ and also $N_{t''}q_{t'}$, where that q at t' is the factor which necessitates that p at t—and which was perhaps itself necessitated by that r at t''. One can then speak of a chain of necessitation or causal chain from the coming true of that r at t'' to the coming true of that p at t.

Can such a chain go back in time indefinitely? I shall here only say that I cannot think of any obvious hindrance of a logical (conceptual) nature to this possibility. An argued answer, positive or negative, would have to consider the nature of time and the relation between time and causality.

The relation of necessitation, as we have defined it here, is *not* transitive. The fact that it was necessary from t' on that p at t and that the necessitating factor was itself necessary from t'' on $(t'' \leqslant t')$ does not entail that it was, in fact, necessary that p at t already from t'' on, because the necessitating effect of a factor depends also on "accompanying circumstances". The necessitating effect of the proposition that q may depend upon an accidental change in the circumstances which happened only after the assumed "cause of the cause", the proposition that r, had come true.

Consider again our example of the man who died in an explosion. The explosion caused his death because he happened to be where he was (in the "fatal area") when the explosion took place. He was already there before the explosion happened. But the explosion, let us assume, had itself a cause which had been there since a time when the man either had not yet entered the area or was in the area but could have escaped from it. Then it would not be right to say that he was "doomed", that is, his death in the explosion necessary, from the time when the cause of the explosion operated.

Thus a chain of necessitating causes of something may go back even infinitely in time (to "the dawn of creation"), and yet the occurrence of that thing have been necessary for a much shorter time, maybe only from the time of the occurrence of its "proximate" necessitating cause. This is so because the causal relation of necessitation normally obtains only within a frame of accompanying circumstances. Some of these circumstances may obtain of natural necessity when the necessitating factor appears; but whether they obtain contingently or of necessity, *their* presence or absence is *independent* of the necessitating factor.

Generally speaking, if the operation of (some) necessitating factors in an unending chain of causes and effects depends on circumstances which are contingent relative to those factors, the relation of necessitation in the chain is not transitive and therefore the necessity of the eventual effect was not there from the appearance of the remotest cause in the chain.

In view of these observations it becomes pertinent to ask: *can* an individual proposition that p at t be in the *strong* sense antecedently necessary, i.e. necessary "from the dawn of creation"?

XIII

Strong necessity is the dual of weak possibility. It is in the weak sense possible that p at t if, at some time before t, it was possible that p at t (although this possibility may, but need not, subsequently have got lost). Let it be that at t' it was possible that p at t. On the elucidation we gave on p. 120 above, this means that no law of nature, under the circumstances prevailing in the interval from t' to t, prevents the proposition that p from coming true at t. Therefore, if the proposition that p at t is *not* in the weak sense possible, i.e. is in the strong sense impossible (its negation necessary), then there is a law of nature which, in spite of all the variations in circumstances which may have taken place since the "beginning" of time, prevents the proposition that p from coming true at t.

Can such a thing be the case? It is surely a *strange* possibility to consider.

If this were the case with the proposition that p at t, would it not also then be the case with this proposition at any other time as well? So that, because of a law of nature, the (generic) proposition that p could never have a true instantiation. Because how could there be a law which is so "sensitive" to variations in circumstances over periods of time which are infinitely long (assuming that time has no real "beginning") that, because of this law, it must be false that p at t, but not necessarily at other times? To maintain that there existed such a law would be tantamount to maintaining that its "decree" about what was going to happen to p at t is *independent* of circumstances. The law itself would be that it is false that p at (just) t—and saying this would be to state a fact and not to enunciate any law at all.

To maintain that an individual proposition is in the strong sense antecedently necessary is thus to make it into a law announcing its own truth. The only way in which this can be done without triviality is, it seems, by extending the law to all instantiations of the corresponding *generic* proposition.

Assume then that the generic proposition that p has no true instantiation, i.e. that the proposition that not-p has only true instantiations, is universal. I tried to argue earlier (above pp. 106ff) that this, i.e. the proposition that the generic proposition is universal, is *true* only if the generic proposition is logically necessary (its contradictory logically impossible). If the proposition that p is logically impossible then it makes no sense to *attribute* its permanent falsehood to a "law of nature". The proposition that it is always the case that not-p might, however, itself be a "law of nature". If we treat it as a synthetic generalization it is either false or has no truth-value. If we exempt it from falsification it is "analytic", i.e. a logical necessity. As we shall see later (p. 139), it is characteristic of laws of nature that they allow these two attitudes to be taken to them.

The generic proposition could, of course, be a molecular compound of some other generic propositions. It might, for example, be the disjunction of the propositions that not-q and that r. In symbols: $\sim q \vee r$ or, which is the same, $q \rightarrow r$. Then the strong antecedent necessity would be that a certain disjunctive state of affairs obtains and the law, warranting this, would be simply the law which says that this is always so independently of "accompanying circumstances". This would correspond to a well-known view of what "laws of nature" in fact are; *viz.* universal implications. It does not mean that the law itself is a natural necessity—only that its instances are in the strong sense antecedently necessary. Whether there *are* any such laws is, however, doubtful (see below, pp. 142f).

Laws of Nature

What is a "law of nature"? Various aspects of the problem will be discussed in the present essay but no exhaustive and final answer will be attempted. The selection of aspects for discussion will, moreover, be linked to what has been said earlier about logical and natural modality.

"Primitive" laws say, for example, that heating water makes it boil, heating a metal rod makes it expand, heating a piece of wax makes it melt, etc. These are typically of the kind: something causing something else. The causing thing is some event or process, and the same holds true of the effect. We have come to know the law from having observed a certain regularity under familiar, frequently recurring circumstances. "Disturbances" sometimes occur, but not too often. Familiarity with disturbances enables us to explain why the law does not always "work"; for example that poor fuel will not engender a sufficiently hot flame for melting a piece of metal. The disturbing factors then work in accordance with other "primitive" laws; otherwise one could not ascribe the disturbances to a specific factor. It is important, moreover, that we should be able to control, and thereby also exclude, at least many such disturbances. If disturbances were frequent and unpredictable, the primary primitive law itself would "collapse". We should perhaps speak of it as a "hypothesis" which was "falsified", or as a "mere" statistical regularity. When sticking to the law we treat it like something which could be called a "quasi-analytic" truth: this process always results in ... *unless disturbed* (cf. later p. 138).

There is an analogy, worth noticing, between the way such primitive laws are enunciated and the way we talk about human actions and their results. The causally efficacious process is characterized in terms of its resulting effect: "boiling water", "melting wax", etc. The process is *that* process the undisturbed, efficacious course of which terminates in, say, that water in a kettle starts boiling; just as the successful performance of the action of shutting a window will *of logical necessity* result in the window being shut.

A closer, more systematic, study of the natural processes—typically undertaken in the form of *experiments*—may reveal further features about the regularities of causal efficacy. We notice, for example, that the change in length of a metal rod when heated has a characteristic "expansion quotient", or that the melting point of wax is such and such, or that increase in atmospheric pressure under constant temperature affects the volume of a gas in a certain way. A new level of "laws of nature" is then reached. Our understanding of the "circumstances" under which we claim validity for the laws, keeping under control possible "disturbances", is also deepened, and becomes more exact. When formulating a law we may then "take it for granted" that, say, atmospheric pressure is "normal" or that friction or the resistance of the medium can be "ignored". We also come to entertain various useful "fictions" such as that the mass of an extended solid body can be regarded as "concentrated" in its point of gravity, etc.

In the course of such study a "scientific" understanding of natural processes gradually emerges. The formulation of laws at the "textbook level" which has now been reached is very different from the formulation of the "primitive" laws. Examples would be the Boyle–Mariotte gas law, Snell's law for the refraction of light, Galileo's laws of falling bodies, or the Proust–Lavoisier law of constant proportions in chemistry. The recording of the melting and boiling points and specific weights of various stuffs may also be counted as belonging to this level of formulation of laws of nature.

There are still many higher levels in the edifice of science. On them a *systematization* of the laws takes place. Inferior laws are "derived" from higher laws. The latter are often principles by virtue of which a whole bundle of previously discovered laws become "unified" in one comprehensive "theory". Newton's law of gravitation is the paradigm example.

The higher we ascend in this hierarchy, the farther are we removed from the actuality of causally interrelated events and processes. At the scientific level, laws of nature are, on the whole, not "causal laws". It was presumably this observation which led Russell in a famous essay to maintain that causality is not prominent in science, the causal laws of our pre-scientific understanding of nature being replaced by functional relationships between quantitatively estimable or measurable variables.[1]

Russell's view has been disputed, and it has also been maintained that the role of causality in theoretical physics is more prominent today than it was at the time when Russell wrote his essay.[2] This may be so—at least if one broadens the notion to what is nowadays often spoken of as statistical or probabilistic causality. We need not go into this controversy here. That *something* was correct in Russell's evaluation of the position of causal laws in science seems to me undeniable.

---

[1] "On the Notion of Cause", *Proceedings of the Aristotelian Society* **XIII** (1912–13); reprinted in *Mysticism and Logic and Other Essays*, Longmans, Green & Co., London, 1918.

[2] See Patrick Suppes, *A Probabilistic Theory of Causality*, North-Holland Publishing Co., Amsterdam, 1970, pp. 5f (*Acta Philosophica Fennica*, fasc. XXIV).

But Russell, and perhaps some of his critics too, neglected one aspect of the situation. There is, after all, a connection from the higher levels of scientific theory down to the basis of natural phenomena the interrelations of which were first laid down in "primitive" laws, often or perhaps usually of a "causal" character.

Consider the "functional relationship" which the gas law in its classic form establishes between the volume, temperature, and (external and internal) pressure of a gas. It does not mention cause and effect. It could perhaps not, or not easily, be formulated as a causal law. But it enables us to predict that a certain determinate change in, say, pressure together with a not-change in temperature will call forth, produce, a determinate change in the volume of a gas in a container. This relation between changes (events in nature) is a good example of a causal relation.

Or consider the "law", itself of a rather "primitive" kind, which says that the melting point of phosphorus is 44°C. What has it to do with causality? Roughly the following: if a piece of phosphorus is, "under appropriate circumstances", heated it will melt, and the melting will start when the temperature of the piece attains 44°C. The heating process acts as cause of the melting process which is the effect. The "appropriate" circumstances are conditions which must be satisfied if the source of heating, say a burning lamp, is to generate a steady increase in temperature of the stuff, and if a correct estimate of the temperature is to be made. Anybody trained to perform elementary chemical experiments will know which these circumstances are, and probably also alternative ways of securing that they obtain; to produce a detailed description of them may be quite laborious, and does not count as belonging to the formulation of the "law of nature" itself.

II

To say that the logically contingent proposition that *p* at *t* is a natural or physical necessity means, we have said (above, p. 120), that there is a law of nature *L* such that, under the then prevailing circumstances *C*, it is necessary that *p* at *t*. In order for this to be consonant with what has been said before about the meaning of the symbol $N_t p_t$—laying aside some doubtful or eccentric cases such as "spontaneous creation of natural necessity"—it is required that the circumstances *C* include what I have called a necessitating factor, say that *q*, antecedent to or perhaps simultaneous with that *p* at *t*. Between the law *L* the occurrence of this necessitating factor, and the rest of the circumstances, call them "*C'*", as antecedents and the proposition that *p* at *t* as consequent there is a relation of (logically) necessary implication. For the sake of simplicity I shall here assume that the occurrence of the necessitating factor is simultaneous with the coming true of that p at t. Thus we have $N(L \ \& \ q_t \ \& \ C' \to p_t)$.

The relation under which the law and the circumstances confer natural or physical necessity on the proposition that p at t is thus itself a relation of necessary implication. This second necessity is not physical but *logical*. It is a species of the relation which modal logicians call "strict implication".

The relation will be assumed to obey the received laws of a "normal" modal logic. Then the antecedent $L \ \& \ C_t$ (or $L \ \& \ q_t \ \& \ C'_t$) cannot be itself logically necessary, since that p at t is assumed to be logically contingent. From this again it follows logically that L and C_t cannot both be necessary but that one of the two *may* be necessary. The possibility that the circumstances C_t were necessary seems out of question; one would rather think of them as being "eminently" contingent. But the possibility that the law L itself is necessary is left open. (It should be remembered that talk of necessity and contingency here refers to the *logical* modalities; C_t may contain many factors, or even only factors, which are themselves *physically* necessary.)

Physical necessity, one could thus say, is a characteristic "combination" of logical necessity and logical contingency (and the same holds good, *mutatis mutandis*, for the other natural modalities). In the elucidation given, however, the notion of a law (of nature) is involved—and the question may be raised whether *it* can be clarified without recourse to notions of modality other than the logical ones. It is a well-known opinion that the laws of nature themselves are a kind of natural or physical necessities. I think this opinion is wrong—contrary to what I have tended to think myself at times in the past. The notion of a "law" is involved in our thinking of some facts of nature as ("natural") necessities; but the notion of *natural* necessity is not itself needed for the purpose of elucidating the concept of a law of nature. The concept of *logical* necessity, however, has a characteristic role to play in connection with natural laws. We already briefly touched upon this in our discussion earlier of the truth of generalizations from experience (p. 108), and more will now have to be said about this.

III

In the early part of our century it was a widely accepted opinion among philosophers of science that the *semper et ubique* of the laws of nature was the result of a conceptual stipulation or convention. The truth of laws of nature was analytical and not synthetical, and the necessity attaching to them resembled logical rather than natural necessity. The position was known as conventionalism and is commonly associated with the great name of Henri Poincaré. Several of its early proponents were French philosophers of science of that time, such as G. Milhaud[3] and Eduard Le Roy.[4] A similar position was held by another French philosopher, now undeservedly forgotten it seems to me—*viz.* Emile Meyerson.[5]

One of the stock examples, brought up for the first time, I think, by Milhaud in an article in *Revue de Metaphysique et de Morale* but also discussed by Poincaré in his works *La Valeur de la Science* and *Science et Méthode*,[6] concerns the melting point of phosphorus. Phosphorus melts at 44°C. This may be called a "law of nature" (cf. above). It says that anything which falls logically in the range of the predicate "phosphorus" either is *not* phosphorus or, if subjected to heating, will melt at 44°C. *This* is a "disjunctive state of affairs" which, according to the law, universally obtains. What now, if a lump of a stuff which we take to be phosphorus does not melt at this temperature when heated? Has the law then been falsified? This conclusion would hardly be drawn at once. Perhaps the melting was not done and the temperature measured under "appropriate conditions" or with "due care". Maybe the measuring instruments were defective or our reading of them inaccurate. Perhaps the lump we melted was not "pure" phosphorus but also contained particles of other substances. Or maybe it was, contrary to appearances, not phosphorus at all. Which characteristics *define* phosphorus; which are the criteria for deciding whether something is phosphorus or not? Here the conventionalist move of thought is to suggest that the melting point itself might be such a criterion. A substance which does not melt at 44°C simply *is not* phosphorus. The "law" is in fact a *standard* for judging whether something is phosphorus or not; therefore its validity is a "necessity" and not a "contingency". But one could also say that, as a standard or stipulation, it is neither true nor false. Definitions are like *norms*. *They are fiats* of language (terminology). As such they lack truth-value. It is necessarily true that phosphorus melts at 44°C, if "phosphorus" *means* "stuff which ... and melts at 44°C". But that "phosphorus" has this meaning, is, *as a stipulation*, neither true nor false.

---

[3] "La science rationelle", *Revue de Métaphysique et de Morale*, **4**, 1896.

[4] "Science et Philosophie", *Revue de Métaphysique et de Morale*, **7**, 1899 and **8**, 1900; also "Sur la logique de l'invention", *ibid.*, **13**, 1915.

[5] *Identité et Réalité*, Félix Alcan, Paris, 1908, and *De l'explication dans les sciences*, Payot, Paris, 1921.

[6] *La Valeur de la Science*, Flammarion, Paris 1904, pp. 235ff.; *Science et Méthode*, Flammarion, Paris, 1908, p. 189f.

In this way of arguing there is much which is sound—provided we do not try to raise it to the level of a universally valid doctrine about the nature of all natural laws. The point of the argument, I should say, is not really one concerning the truth or universal validity of the isolated statement that phosphorus melts at such and such a temperature. It is rather one about the position of this statement in a much broader context of chemical and physical theory. To doubt a well-established opinion about the fixed melting point of a given substance is a serious step which we are reluctant to take and for the avoidance of which the concrete situation offers a number of loop-holes of which *one*, among many, is of the type "this cannot have been phosphorus, since it did not melt at the 'right' temperature". But whether we resort to this loop-hole or to some other, such as for example doubting the instruments of measurement, or whether we let the experiment "falsify" the law, or whether we just lay aside the case as one with which we do not know how to deal—this will be decided by considerations for which no general rules can be laid down once and for all. And therefore the answer to the question whether the statement that phosphorus melts at 44°C is analytic or synthetic is that in some (experimental) situations we *treat* it as analytic and necessary, in some others as synthetic and possibly false—but that in most situations the question simply does not arise.[7]

This "open" character of laws of nature with regard to the synthetic–analytic, and therewith also the contingent–necessary, dimension is a feature of thesis which justifies us in saying that they are either false, *viz.* when (clearly) contradicted by the established truth of some individual proposition, or else neither true nor false (see above, p. 110).

IV

We shall now consider the role which the circumstances C prevailing at t play in conferring, together with the law L, contingent necessity on a proposition of the form that p at t. As our example we shall continue to use the proposition about the melting point of phosphorus.

Imagine the following situation. We have a specimen of a substance which we are certain is phosphorus. In order to be certain we ascertained this—perhaps relying on external characteristics or perhaps on some experimental tests we made. The details of how we arrived at this certainty

---

[7] For a discussion of the conventionalist point of view in the philosophy of science the reader is referred to my early work *The Logical Problem of Induction*, 2nd rev. edn., Basil Blackwell, Oxford, 1957, pp. 40–53 and 195–8.

need not concern us here. Only this is important: we did *not* use the melting point as a criterion. We now start to heat the substance under conditions which, we are certain, satisfy the requirements of a scientific experiment as far as control of external influences, apparell, and skill in performing the experiment is concerned. We take it for granted, moreover, that phosphorus melts at 44°C. We therefore predict that when the temperature of the substance reaches 44°C, the substance will change its state of aggregation from solid to liquid. Considering the basis for our prediction we may say, moreover, that this, under the circumstances, is necessary. Perhaps we can calculate when the critical temperature is reached and the melting process will start. Thus we may already say when the experiment is "put on" that it is certain or necessary that at such and such a time the melting of the substance will occur.

Assume that the melting happens as predicted. The outcome of the experiment then gave us no reason for doubting either that the substance was phosphorus or that phosphorus melts at 44°C. Unless we happen to have some independent reason for doubting either of these two things we might say that the melting of the substance then was a necessity under natural law. There is no need now to look closer into the circumstances under which the melting took place.

Assume, however, that things do not go as predicted. This *may* afford a reason for doubting whether, after all, phosphorus melts at the temperature in question. More likely, it will make us suspect either that the substance we melted was not a "pure" specimen of phosphorus, or that the temperature had not been correctly measured, or that something had intervened which "disturbed" the process—for example a sudden change in atmospheric pressure. Like the law itself, the circumstances under which it is being applied in a concrete situation also have an "openness" which makes it impossible to specify *exactly* beforehand what must be included in the clause *C* in order to make the predicted event follow of necessity from the law under those circumstances. This open character of the circumstances is reflected in a *façon de parler* familiar both from experimental practice and from writings on the philosophy of science, *viz.* the following:

One says that if the law is well confirmed and established, then *ceteris paribus* it will hold good in this case too. "Ceteris paribus" literally means "other things being equal". Obviously, the circumstances C_t vary from case to case, i.e. vary with the value of t or of an interval $t' - t$. The demand of constancy inherent in the *ceteris paribus* clause can concern only such factors which are relevant to the validity (applicability) of L, i.e. the presence or absence of which is required in the individual case in order to warrant the contingent necessity of the proposition that p_t. Such factors can also be said to *condition* or to *restrict* the applicability of the law.

Some such factors may be well known and their due presence or absence presupposed in the individual case. For example: Pure alcohol starts boiling when heated to about 80°C. But this certainly is not an unconditional truth. A condition is that the atmospheric pressure be "normal". One can work this condition into the formulation of the "law" and say that pure alcohol under normal pressure boils at 80°C; or one could aim at formulating a more *general* law which makes the boiling point a *function* of the atmospheric pressure under which the heating of the liquid takes place.

Of a similar but not identical nature is the case when the validity of the law is restricted to certain "ideal" circumstances which we know are *not* satisfied in the individual situations to which the law is applied. Laws of how bodies move under the impact of forces may be subject to a clause "ignoring the resistance of the medium" or "ignoring friction". By taking into account the factors which are deliberately excluded from the "ideal" circumstances one may be able to state a *compound* law which approximates more closely to the "real" circumstances of the law's applications.

Now one may ask: is it possible through successive stages of *generalization* and *approximation* to "drain" the *ceteris paribus* clause of *all* factors which are relevant to the deduction of the proposition that p_t from the law L? The question means the following:

Can the law be stated in such a form $\wedge (q \rightarrow p)$ that the only "part" of C_t which is relevant to the contingent necessity that p_t is the "part" that q_t? (Above, p. 133).

The answer is Yes. One can do this by "freezing" the formulation of the law into a standard of its own truth, i.e. by making the law "analytic". Then, if it was *thought to be* the case that q_t and also that $\sim p_t$, one would have to conclude that, "after all", it either *was not* the case that q_t ("the substance cannot have been phosphorus") or *was* the case that p_t ("either the temperature was less than 44°C *or* the substance was actually melting"). The only circumstances which enter the picture are now the identification of the substance as phosphorus, its state of aggregation, and the temperature. Everything else is "by definition" irrelevant.

But suppose an examination of the case gives us no reason for thinking that either $\sim q_t$ or p_t. This would normally be grounds for abandoning the idea of the law as a standard and for taking a second look at the circumstances C_t in order to see whether there may not have been missing from them some factor such that, only when *it* is not there, is that q_t connected by natural law with that p_t. Perhaps this factor had always before been present, but we had failed to take notice of it or to think that its presence was relevant. Call this factor r. One could lift it out from C_t and include it in L which would now state that $\wedge(q \ \& \ r \rightarrow p)$. The law, thus reformulated, we may again "freeze" into an analytic truth. But nothing can assure us once and for all that we shall not be confronting a new situation which gives us a reason for abandoning the adopted standard. As long as we retain an "open mind" with a view to this possibility, we cannot be sure that our attitude to the law will not change in future. Only through an act of decision, therefore, can the *ceteris paribus* clause which goes with a law of nature be "drained" of all factors which are relevant—and thereby itself be reduced to irrelevance.

V

What shall we say of the logical form of laws of nature in view of this account of the role of the circumstances C in conferring contingent necessity on the proposition that p_t? Is this form, or is it not, that of a universal implication?

"Phosphorus melts at 44°C." Is this not a shorthand way of saying that if something is a piece of phosphorus then it will melt at 44°C? And is this not meant to be a universal generalization, valid for *all* pieces of phosphorus? More than this, is it not really a statement about "everything there is" or at least about everything in the *range* of the property of being a piece of phosphorus? Because does it not say that it is true of everything that either it is *not* a piece of phosphorus *or* it melts at 44°C?

If these last questions are taken seriously, I think the answer to them is No. "The melting point of phosphorus is 44°C" associates a characteristic with a certain type of material, phosphorus. The substance "as such" cannot be melted, but pieces of it, when subject to heating, will melt at a temperature of 44°C. As it stands "if this is a piece of phosphorus, it will melt at 44°C" need not even be true. The piece may never be subjected to melting, so to improve the sentence one would have to add to it a clause "if heated under appropriate circumstances"—a formulation which certainly is both incomplete and unperspicuous unless we specify the "appropriate circumstances" in detail.

In books on science, laws are seldom if ever stated in the form of universal implications. Giving them this form is, at best, a reformulation; but normally it is also an oversimplification—and, at worst, a distortion of their content.

The discrepancy between the text-book formulation and the various attempts at making the structure of laws explicit in the terms of formal logic is, I think, significant. The text-book formulation is indeed a shorthand; but not merely for the universal implication which usually may, without much ado, be "extracted" from it. That phosphorus melts at 44°C means, we have said, that if something is a piece of phosphorus then it will melt, if "under appropriate conditions" heated to 44°C. Which the "appropriate conditions" are, under which the heating has to take place, is not spelt out in the standard formulation of the law. It is partly implicit in the background knowledge which anybody who handles the law for predicting the outcome of an experiment or process is assumed to possess. But there is also an open margin for new conditions to be imposed—for example in cases which involve the use of unfamiliar experimental techniques. One can say that the standard formulation of the law *conceals* the open character of the conditions of its application, whereas the *reformulation* of the law as a universal implication just *cuts out* these circumstances by giving to the law a sharp logical structure which it does not "in itself" possess.

When therefore, in an individual case, we pronounce it contingently necessary that p_t, we do not only deduce this proposition *modo ponente* from an implication the antecedent of which is instantiated at t. We also take it for granted that this implication instantiates a law the conditions of application of which are satisfied. The statement of contingent necessity thus has an epistemic component which defies generalization and ties the validity of the statement to the concrete situation.

Wittgenstein speaks in his *Remarks on the Foundations of Mathematics* about "der unheilvolle Einbruch der Logik in die Mathematik" ("the disastrous intrusion of logic into mathematics").[8] What he meant by this we need not stop to consider here. But I think one could make a parallel remark—perhaps even more justified—and speak of the "disastrous intrusion of symbolic logic into writings on the philosophy of science". By this I mean that use of logical symbolism easily has a corrupting influence on philosophic thinking about the sciences in that it forces the conceptual structures involved in scientific thinking and scientific experimenting into a Procrustean bed from which we must lift them out if we are to see them clearly in their complexity and fullness.

VI

I have argued that any statement to the effect that something or other is contingently necessary involves an existential statement to the effect that there is (exists) a law L such that ... Our next question is: what is the

---

[8] *Bemerkungen über die Grundlagen der Mathematik—Remarks on the Foundations of Mathematics*, Suhrkamp Verlag, Frankfurt am Main, 1974; Basil Blackwell, Oxford, 1978, p. 281; see also *ibid.*, pp. 299 and 300.

mode of existence which laws have? What does it mean that a law of nature "exists"?

The existence of a law of nature is not a "fact" in the same sense as the obtaining of a state of affairs or the occurrence of an event is a fact.

One cannot disentangle the existence of laws from considerations of an epistemic nature. To say that there is a law such that . . . is *like* saying that we have a "device" or "method" or "formula" for *predicting* that *p* at *t* under some circumstances and for *explaining* why *p* at *t* once this is an established fact. We *know how* to do this.

But is this not to confuse the existence of the law with our claim to know it? Most laws are *discovered* thanks to experiments and observations. Did they not exist before they were discovered? Assume that we had witnessed in the past that *q* at *t'* and that *p* at *t* without seeing that these facts are "connected". Then a law is found such that, under given circumstances (as known to us), that *p* at *t* becomes deducible from that *q* at *t'*. Would we not then say, in retrospect, that whenever in the past it was the case that *q* under similar circumstances, it was also contingently necessary that *p*? Of course we would do this. So did the law not "exist" then, before it was discovered? The question is confusing. It is a characteristic of laws that they should be valid *semper et ubique*. But this does not mean that they have a permanence in time—like an object which never breaks or perishes. That we have found a law means that we have become able to *connect in our understanding* facts (events) which previously did not seem to us connected. Such a change in our understanding is sometimes made possible because new facts come to light which serve as "links" between facts hitherto disconnected, but sometimes also because we relate the facts to some already found ("existing") law about cases which initially looked different. (Analogies, isomorphisms, "seeing familiar things in a new light".) The acquired new insight of ours we then use for purposes of predicting facts of the future and explaining facts of the past or present. This is what the "semper et ubique" means. Not to take *it* for granted is to profess doubts whether we have found the law yet or are only making tentative efforts to formulate it correctly.

I think it was a deep insight, expressed perhaps for the first time with greatest clarity by David Hume, that causal connections—and nomic (lawful) connections generally—are not existents at the level of particulars, like a glue which keeps things tied together, "out there" in nature, independent of the mind. Hume would have said that there is no "impression" corresponding to the connection between cause and effect. This does not mean, however, that the laws of nature were "creations of the mind". Because both their discovery and successful handling for purposes of prediction and explanation *depend* upon facts of nature. But if we had to "locate" their existence at all—which is not necessary—it seems to me less misleading to say that laws exist *in our understanding* than saying that they exist *in nature*. (This point is related, I believe, to what Kant meant by his "Copernican revolution" in epistemology.)

Scientists are in search of the laws of nature. The faith in the success of their pursuit is a faith in the powers of the human understanding—coupled with a belief or an expectation that facts which have not yet come to our notice will be discovered and enable us to see an order where before we saw none. To say that there is, or must be, a law where none has yet been found is therefore an existential statement only in the sense that it expresses our faith or hope that some day we shall understand what is for the time being obscure.

VII

I said earlier (p. 55) that knowledge of laws of nature should not count as genuine "knowledge of the future". The reasons for holding this opinion are, I think, plain from what has already been said. But it is worth reviewing now in the light of the more general question whether, and in what sense, laws of nature can be objects of knowledge at all.

Positivists, at least those of a sceptical turn of mind, would deny that laws of nature can be known to be true. Their argument draws on the anticipatory character of laws, the fact that they "transcend" the body of ascertainable facts and cover an (in principle) unlimited number of unexamined future (and also past) instances. Since they cannot be strictly verified, laws of nature, unless made true by convention, are *hypotheses* and as such open to future refutation (falsification).

It would be part and parcel of positivist scepticism that the future cannot be known—and that therefore laws of nature because they reach out into the future cannot be objects of knowledge—only of belief and conjecture. With this part of the positivists' argument I disagree. It *is* also possible to know things which are not yet there but are going to be—and I hope I have argued for this convincingly. But at the same time there is something in the positivist attitude with which I am in deep sympathy, *viz. that* aspect of the view of some of them which I have tried to articulate in my thesis that non-logical universal generalizations are either false or else void of truth-value, neither true nor false. If we take this view, it follows at once that laws of nature cannot be known in that sense of "know" which means knowing that something is true (or is the case). Since knowledge in that sense entails truth—and if a proposition is such that it is either false or void of truth-value it cannot, for plain logical reasons, be *known to be true*. Laws of nature, other than those which may be necessary truths, are not contingent in the normal sense of that term which means possibly true and possibly false—and therefore there is no knowing their (contingent) truth either.

However, both the sceptics' view and the view of those logical positivists who thought that non-logical generalizations are neither true nor false seem to conflict with the way we commonly talk and think about these things. I presume that scientists who have reflected about the epistemology of their subject would admit that a good many generalizations in science are ("only") hypotheses awaiting (further) confirmation or (eventual) refutation, and perhaps also that some are "true by convention". But they would surely think, most of them at least, that there exists a solid body of established scientific knowledge which is by no means confined to singular observations or outcomes in experiments, but must be regarded as "theoretical" insights into the working of the "forces" and "mechanisms" of nature.

How is this "conflict" between the sceptic and the reflective scientist to be resolved? By taking notice, I think, of the logically open character of the laws and of their conditions of application. This openness is reflected in the epistemological status of the laws as follows:

Through observations and carefully designed experiments we have discovered or established a great many relationships between natural phenomena. These relationships, once well confirmed and tested, find their place in a bulk of what is called—and rightly so, I think—accepted scientific knowledge. They are the "certainties", on the basis of which research progresses—new questions are raised and new relationships discovered. Sometimes these certainties themselves are being questioned, no longer taken for granted—and as a consequence of such questioning we may impose restrictions upon their applicability, for example limit it to situations in which certain factors (friction, resistance of air, electric charge, etc.) are deliberately ignored. Seldom only does such questioning lead to a straightforward "falsification", rejection of that which was once regarded as "common knowledge" in science. The reason we "dare" to speak of this as "knowledge" is partly the necessity of basing new results in science on accepted certainties (otherwise one could hardly speak of the growth of scientific knowledge at all), and partly the existence of the innumerable "loop-holes" for "saving" accepted knowledge from wholesale rejection by means of conditionalizing or restricting the scope of generalizations made.

The question is not really whether we know or can know laws of nature to be *true*. The claim we make to possess knowledge of laws of nature is not a straightforward truth-claim. It is nevertheless a claim which is amply justified on the basis of accumulated knowledge of facts (truths) and of success in using the laws as vehicles for prediction and explanation. Sometimes the claim is challenged for a particular law and will have to be given up or modified—usually because of the acquisition of new knowledge (of truths). As long as it remains uncontested for a particular law, this law is *regarded* or *treated* as belonging to the bulk of accepted scientific knowledge.

Laws of nature, one could say, are kinds of "propositional instruments" which we use for predicting and explaining contingent necessities. Because of their "open" character they are themselves neither necessary nor contingent and their truth cannot therefore be a genuine object of knowledge. "Do you know the gas law?" means "Can you cite it?" or "Do you know how to use it in a certain calculation or construction or experiment?" It does not mean "Do you know whether the gas law is true?" Knowing laws of nature is more like a *know how* than a *know that*. It is the skill of scientists to be able to *handle* them. And as long as they are handled, and not tested, they are treated as the certainties on which science progresses.

VIII

The type of "laws of nature" which I have in the first place had in mind in this discussion can be broadly characterized as "generalizations from experience" or as resting on "inductive evidence" provided by experiments and observations. Statements about the melting and boiling points of various materials, their specific weight and other "macroscopic" properties have this character—and the same would be true of, say, Boyle–Mariotte's Law, of Snell's law of refraction of light, of the Mendelian laws of heredity, and a great many others. But it would certainly not be right to characterize all laws of nature as either "inductive generalizations" with an "open" truth-value, or as generalizations which have been "frozen" into conventions or standards. Many laws—and I presume this holds true without exception of the most "general" or "basic" ones—are better characterized as stating connections within the conceptual framework itself used in describing and interpreting the findings of experiment and observation. They belong to the stage of "systematization" rather than to that of "discovery" in the advancement of scientific knowledge (cf. above, p. 135).

Consider the Law of Inertia, for example. Its acquisition was the result of a gigantic struggle of the human mind for a new conceptual framework of understanding nature which was to replace the Aristotelian framework of late scholasticism. This struggle was, of course, inseparably tied up with a mass of observations and experiments—but it was not a struggle to back a hypothesis by inductive evidence. Within the new frame, eventually established through the work of Newton, the Law of Inertia holds the position of a conceptual truth—to be shaken only by a change in the frame. But changes in the frame such as we have later witnessed are themselves in the last resort prompted by new observations and new experiments which failed to be accommodated within the old frame.

The Law of Inertia which says that a body continues in its state of rest or uniform rectilinear motion unless acted upon by an external force holds in the conceptual frame of classical physics a position *somewhat* similar to certain propositions within the conceptual frame which we use for describing human actions and their relations to a motivational background in the intentional life of man. Consider the following case:

Whenever I decide to raise my arm I do it, unless I am prevented by circumstances "external to my will" or reverse my decision. This is "logically necessary", a conceptual truth. Now assume that I decide to raise my arm; and up it goes, it raises—an event in nature. As shown by the case, I was not disabled or prevented. Under the circumstances the rising of my arm was a contingent necessity. What was contingent about it was that I decided to raise my arm then and that I was not prevented (or reversed my decision). The necessity resided in the *logical* connection between my decision, the circumstances, and my action; but this connection is no guarantee that what I decide will also happen.

The natural event of my arm's rising depended on my decision in much the same sense of "depend" as that in which an effect depends on its cause. But in as much as it was contingent that nothing prevented me from carrying my decision into effect, what happened did *not* depend *on me* (my "will"). I think this is what Wittgenstein meant when he said in the *Tractatus* that "The world is independent of my will" (6.373) and added (6.374) that "Even if everything we wished were to happen, this would only be, so to speak, a favour of fate, for there is no *logical* connection between will and world, which would guarantee this, and the assumed physical connection itself we could not again will."

Perhaps we could extend this argument to an all-powerful decision-maker and say as follows: things happen the way God has ordained. Then also every physical contingency which may intervene and prevent a decision of God's from being carried into effect would depend on his decision (and its occurrence therefore be tantamount to a reversal of his decision). Whether we think that God ever reverses a decision of his or not, the fact remains that everything that happens depends on what God has ordained or decided. *His* decisions would not, like ours, depend on "the favours of fate" for coming true—since these favours themselves are "bestowed" by him. In his case there is a *logical* connection between will and world which guarantees that what he decrees will also be.

I tried to show earlier (p. 67) that the conception of God as an *omniscient* being would not make him, i.e. his knowledge, independent of the world, i.e. of the contingent ways of things. But the conception of God as *omnipotent* anchors the way things go in him. One could call the conception of God as omniscient "intellectualist" and the conception of him as omnipotent "voluntarist"; and I am inclined to say that only the second is a *religious* conception of God.

Subject Index

ability 66
action 57, 65ff, 134, 148f
affirmation 42f
alethic logic, *see* truth-logic
analytic (truth) 133, 137ff
antinomy (antinomic proposition)
 40f

becoming 37ff, 82
bivalence, law of 2ff, 10f, 20,
 32f, 35f, 52, 112

causal
 chain 93ff, 131f
 connection 93f
 efficacy 80, 82ff
 knowledge 59, 86–95
 relation, *see* causation
causation (causality) 76f, 79ff,
 82ff, 86ff, 118, 134ff
 see also cause
 instantaneous (simultaneous)
 124, 127f
cause 76f, 82ff, 91, 93, 123ff,
 127ff
 see also causation
certain(ty) 8f, 53, 57, 60, 71, 88,
 92, 146f
ceteris paribus 92, 140ff
change 37, 39, 56, 78, 82ff, 90,
 92
change in modal status, *see*
 modality; necessitation
circumstances (accompanying)
 83ff, 88ff, 120f, 123ff, 130ff,
 135ff
 see also ceteris paribus

condition 79f, 91
 see also causation
conditional 92ff
consequentia mirabilis 40f
contingency (contingent) 1, 3,
 55f, 65, 67, 68–71, 79, 96f,
 100, 115, 121f, 136f
contingency clause 125f
 see also ceteris paribus
contingent necessity, *see* necessity
contradiction 2, 4
 law of 35f, 38f
conventionalism 137ff
counterfactual conditional, *see*
 conditional

denial 42f
destroying 82
determinism vii, 2f, 11, 52–67,
 74f, 85, 95, 122
dialectical logic viii, 36, 39
dialectical synthesis 36–9
disjunction 27
disjunctive state of affairs 58,
 133, 138

excluded middle, law of 2f, 10f,
 32f, 38f, 52, 112f
existence, *see* quantification
experiment 89, 93, 134f
explanation 58, 144, 147

falsehood viii, 2, 25, 27, 38,
 42, 108
 see also negation
falsification 146

foreknowledge, *see* knowledge of the future
free will   52, 65ff
   see also action
future   1, 10, 92
   knowledge of, *see* knowledge
future contingency   3f, 11

generalization   50f, 108ff, 133, 137, 141, 145, 147
generic (event, level, proposition, state), *see* proposition
God   52f, 61, 64ff, 68ff, 148f
   see also omniscience and omnipotence
grammatical   6, 19ff, 44
ground, *see* knowledge

Heisenberg's uncertainty relation 37
hypothesis   91, 93, 146ff

implication   15, 18, 136f
induction   86, 147f
introspection   71
intuitionism (intuitionist logic) 34, 47

knowledge   8f, 52ff, 86ff, 145ff
   causal   59, 86−95
   claim to   61ff, 71
   contingent   64, 68
   of the future   52−71, 145
   ground(s) of   53ff
   how   52, 57, 144, 147
   immediate   70f
   impersonal   52f
   of the laws of nature   55
   necessary   68−71
   personal   52f
   that   52, 147
   whether   52, 68ff

law of nature   55, 108ff, 120, 123, 125, 127, 130, 133, 134−49
   existence of   143ff
   form of   133, 141ff
   knowledge of   55, 145ff
liar (paradox of the liar)   40
logic of predication, *see* predication
logic of truth, *see* truth-logic
logical positivism   18, 23, 108f, 119f, 145f

many-valued logic   4
master argument   ix, 75
mean(ing)   14ff, 108f
meaningless   18ff, 23, 43, 108ff
modality   96−103, 104−16, 117−33
   causal, *see* modality, natural
   diachronic   9f, 74, 97ff, 104, 118, 128, 130
   Diodorean   73ff, 118ff
   logical   104−16, 118, 137
   modal status   104ff, 119, 121, 129ff
   natural   117−33, 137
   physical, *see* modality, natural
   prospective   97, 102, 118, 120
   retrospective   98, 118, 120, 124, 126
   Russell's view of   105f, 110, 116, 119
   statistical interpretation of   73
   synchronic   74, 96ff, 104, 118, 128, 130
modal logic   68f, 137
modal status, *see* modality

necessitation   121, 123ff, 129ff, 136

necessity   8ff, 68–71, 136
   antecedent   74, 96ff, 121ff
   atemporal   72f, 117
   contingent   55, 70, 101, 139f,
      147
   of the factual   76
   logical   69f, 137, 148f
   natural   69f, 137
   of the past   75, 98, 118, 120
   physical, *see* necessity, natural
   of the present   72, 98, 118, 120
   simpliciter   72f, 75
   spontaneous origination of
      130, 136
   strong   100f, 121f, 132f
   and truth   9f, 111ff
   and universality   105ff
   weak   100f, 121f, 126
   see also contingency
negation   viif, 2, 34f, 42f
   of a property   42f

omnipotence   149
omniscience   52f, 61, 64ff, 68ff,
   149
omnitemporal(ity)   7, 73, 105f
opportunity (for action)   66
oracle   59ff

plenitude, principle of   106ff,
   110, 119
possibility   74f, 96, 106, 119ff,
   126
   antecedent   96ff
   spectrum of   97ff
   strong   100f
   weak   100f
possible world(s)   73, 97, 106f
possible worlds semantics   73
predetermination (predetermined)
   2, 52ff, 74f, 98
see also determinism

predication   42–51
prediction   144, 147
prevention (preventing)   77ff,
   82–5
process   37ff, 56
production (producing)   77, 80f,
   82–5
property   42ff
proposition   6f, 14–25, 105, 117
   existential   24
   generic   7, 24f, 55, 104f, 110f,
      117f, 121f
   individual   7, 24f, 55, 104f,
      111, 117, 121f
   and sentence   6f, 14ff
   universal   24, 105ff

quantification   44–51

reason(s)   58, 66, 87
refer(ence)   16, 22

salva veritate   4, 12
sea battle   1ff
semper et ubique   105, 137, 144
sempiternal, *see* omnitemporal
sentence   6f, 14ff
   closed   24, 44f
   constative (declarative)   21
   descriptive   22
   open   24, 44f
   prescriptive use of   22
   subject-predicate   43ff, 48f;
      see also predication
      see also proposition
state (of affairs), *see* proposition
system   90

tautology   28, 33ff
   see also truth-tautology
teleology   81f
that(-clause)   21

theory 89
three-valued logic 31f
time 76ff, 96ff, 130
  and causality 76ff
time-screen 97ff
token 16f, 22
trust(ing) 53, 60
truth viii, 4ff, 14ff, 26–41,
    111f, 116, 145f
  atemporality of 5ff, 9, 78
  -constituent 30ff
  future 75
  -logic viii, 26–41, 107f, 112f,
    114
  plain 5ff
  sempiternal 7
  spurious 9f
  strict 38
  -tautology 31ff

-value 2f, 5, 12, 18ff, 31ff,
  48, 50f
type 16f, 22

understanding 144f
ungrammatical, *see* grammatical
uniformity (of nature) 57ff, 86,
  88, 91
universal implication 133, 141ff
universality 105–10, 122f

vagueness 39
variable 25, 45
verifiability 23, 108

werden, see becoming
will 148f

Zeno's arrow 36

Index of Persons

Ackrill, J.L. 20
Anscombe, G.E.M. vii, ix
Aquinas, Thomas 72
Aristotle vii, ix, 1, 3, 4, 20, 32,
    42, 72–7, 81, 98, 118, 120

Baker, G.P. 109
Becker, O. 73
Boethius 72, 73
Braithwaite, R.B. 18, 109
Broad, C.D. 14, 16, 18
Brouwer, L.E.J. 34, 110

Diamond, C. ix
Diodorus Cronus vii, ix, 73, 75,
    81, 118, 119, 120, 121

Edghill, E.M. 20

Frege, G. 16

Ginet, C. ix
Gödel, K. 19

Halldén, S. viii
Hautamäki, A. viii, 29
Hegel, G.W.F. viii, 37
Hilpinen, R. ix, 75
Hintikka, J. vii, ix, 3, 73
Hume, D. 144

Johnson, W.E. 14, 16
Jordan, Z. 3

Kant, I. 107, 145
Ketonen, O. viii
Keynes, J.N. 16

Kneale, W. & M. 78
Knuuttila, S. 73
Kraft, W. 109

Leibniz, G.W. 73
LeRoy, E. 138
Lewy, C. 17
Lovejoy, A.O. 106
Łukasiewicz, J. 3, 4, 5, 9, 10, 11

McColl, S. 3
McGuinness, B.F. 109
Malcolm, N. ix, 58, 62
Marsh, R. Ch. 16, 105
Meyerson, E. 138
Milhaud, G. 138
Moore, G.E. 8, 14, 17, 18, 19,
    20, 23, 60
Mulder, H. 109

Newton, I. 148
Niiniluoto, I. ix, 75

Ockham, W. 72

Patzig, G. 3
Poincaré, H. 138
Prior, A.N. vii
Provence Hintikka, M.B. ix, 75

Ramsey, F.P. 18, 109
Rand, R. 3
Reichenbach, H. 19
Ross, D. 20
Russell, B. 14–19, 22, 51, 105,
    106, 110, 116, 119, 135, 136

Saarinen, E.   ix, 75
Schilpp, P.A.   19
Schlick, M.   109
Shoemaker, S.   ix
Słupecki, J.   3
Smolenov, Hr.   viii
Suppes, P.   135

Teichman, J.   ix

van de Velde-Schlick, B.F.   109
Vuillemin, J.   vii

Waismann, Fr.   109
Weyl, H.   109, 110
Whitehead, A.N.   16
Wittgenstein, L.   14, 105, 109,
     110, 115, 116, 143, 148

Zeno   36